Town and Country Boy

Donald Munnings

Copyright © 2022 Donald Munnings

All rights reserved. No portion of this book may be reproduced in any form whether physical, electronic, digital, audio or otherwise, without express written permission from the author, except as permitted by copyright law of England and Wales. (Currently the Copyright, Designs and Patents Act 1988)

Contents

Prologue: Grandfather's Fall From Grace 7
Chapter 1: Wartime Streatham.................................. 12
Chapter 2: Tenterden and Other Wild Places 19
Chapter 3: Wheels Without Engines 34
Chapter 4: The Table... 39
Chapter 5: The Parrot Who Taught Father to Swear 44
Chapter 6: Of Ducks and Things................................ 49
Chapter 7: Golden Eagle 54
Chapter 8: Greatstone.. 59
Chapter 9: Beetles.. 67
Chapter 10: Delinquents... 72
Chapter 11: The Dead Pond....................................... 80
Chapter 12: Hospital.. 85
Chapter 13: School in the Morning............................ 92
Chapter 14: The Breton Onion Seller......................... 97
Chapter 15: The Dread Serpent of SW16 102
Chapter 16: Fall... 108
Chapter 17: Room 101.. 113
Chapter 18: A Fourpenny Bus Ride........................... 117
Chapter 19: Model Aircraft.. 122
Chapter 20: The Red Panther.................................... 127
Chapter 21: Austin Ten 132

Chapter 22: Brighton or Bust in Indigo Shorts 137
Chapter 23: Private Water...142
Chapter 24: Four Wheels...147
Chapter 25: Grass Track Racing..................................152
Chapter 26: Tractor 156
Chapter 27: The Triangle 161
Chapter 28: The Boat With No Name 165
Chapter 29: Selling the Boat With No Name 171
Chapter 30: The Herne Bay Car and Boating Years 176
Chapter 31: Back to Freshwater Fishing 181
Chapter 32: Surviving to the New Millennium.......185
Chapter 33: Surviving Retirement..............................190

Prologue: Grandfather's Fall From Grace

I shall start this light-hearted catalogue of events with my maternal grandfather Jacob.

Known as Jaap to his friends and family, he was what is now known as a 'People Person'—something of a Dutch Bon Viveur if such a thing is possible. He was the oldest relative I knew personally, and knew well enough to drink with—my paternal grandparents having died long before I was aware of them.

Jacob had a middle-class background, being the son of a prosperous miller and seed merchant in Haamstede, in the north of the island of Schowen and Duiveland, in Zeeland. Having had a decent education on the mainland and extensive training as a 'Bloemenkweker'—which in English would be a horticulturist or flower grower—he was set for a bright future amongst his extensive family connections in the farming world. Not content with being a flower expert, he also indulged in training horses, with a profitable sideline in buying and selling the noble beasts.

As a member of an amateur singing group (was there no limit to the man's talents?) he performed at a hotel in the biggest town on the island—Zierikzee. The hotelier's name was Adriaan. Before taking up hotel owning, he had previously been a farmer in Goes and before that a miller in Owerkerke. He had a son and four daughters. Jaap was attracted to one of the daughters, named Johanna.

Jaap wooed Johanna, and although a smallish man he was a handsome smooth-tongued devil with the ladies. He sought to win Johanna's hand with or without the approval of her family. Many of them disapproved of him strongly, coming eventually to regard him as a monster until their dying day.

However, marriages between well-known families on the island were considered no bad thing. Johanna, known as Jo, was a tall woman and towered above Jaap, but he never seemed bothered by this. They set up home in a nice house overlooking the inner harbour in Zierikzee, and set about creating a family. Their firstborn was my mother, Johanna Pieternella, who arrived in 1908. Then a son, Adriaan Willem, followed swiftly in 1909. Life was good for them and there were no clouds on the horizon.

In the midst of this domestic bliss and contentment, disaster was to strike after an unfortunate incident involving some horses belonging to Jaap's aunt. It would appear these horses were taken to be sold at the market on the mainland, and Jaap was requested to secure a good deal for her.

There was a large discrepancy between the amount stated on the receipt of sale, and the money the aunt received from Jaap. I find the idea of him stealing very unlikely. He was not stupid, and such an action would have been sure to end in disaster. He was an intelligent, hard-working and scrupulously honest man throughout his life.

Based on half-heard conversations and stories from my mother and aunt, I have pieced together a likely scenario for the fall from grace that was to end in my grandfather, and his little family, having to pack their bags and emigrate to England. How much of the following story is true we will never know, as everyone concerned has been dead for years.

I have to give him the benefit of the doubt on this matter and put it down to a youthful indiscretion cause by a little too much drink.

* * * * * * *

Having risen early, Jaap and his friends led the six horses along the track towards the mainland ferry. The horses were calm and gave no trouble, Jaap himself having overseen their training. He was confident they would get to the port in time to catch the day's first boat to the mainland.

They arrived with time to spare and breakfasted well in the port café. At Jaap's expense of course. Their spirits were high as they herded the horses the hundred yards or so to the boat and safely in to a pen on the deck.

A ferry boat without a bar would be a poor thing, and it would have been rude of Jaap and his little retinue not to give such a place their patronage. So, in spite of the early hour they washed the road-dust from their throats with the first drinks of the day.

Disembarking at the mainland in high spirits, they led the horses the few miles to the market. Where they had a few more drinks while awaiting the start of proceedings.

The horses fetched a good price, further enhancing the group's good humour. Jaap had been promised a generous commission on the sale, so they indulged in a good meal and copious amounts of alcohol. All at Jaap's expense.

There were some mind-bending drinks available in Holland in the early 20th century. They had yet to ban absinthe, and in later years grandfather admitted to me that he had once been partial to it. Grandfather lost control of matters and the party went on late into the night with him having agreed to foot the bill…

He woke the following morning with the mother and father of all headaches in more ways than one. Most of the money received for the horses had been spent and this is where the mystery deepens. It is difficult to believe a man of his varied talents and connections couldn't have raised the money to repay his aunt. Surely the shame felt within his immediate family would have faded eventually.

Perhaps he intended to move to England anyway, and arrangements were already in place. There is no way he could have made the move without a great deal of help from someone, but the details will have to remain a mystery. The fact was that within days he was en-route for England, with a good job and accommodation to go to, and money in his pocket.

My mother, at only two-years-old, was embarking on an epic journey. In a bizarre twist of circumstances thirty years later, I would mirror her seafaring adventure, also at the tender age of two.

The reasons for the repeat journey, this time from Jersey, were somewhat different though, as I shall explain in the first chapter.

****

Recently researching the family history, I managed to identify several elegant photographs. They were taken at the end of the nineteenth century in Holland, and with the help of a cousin over there, I pieced together the fascinating lives my grandparents led before coming to England.

The windmill on the farm in Owerkerk, on the island of Schowen, where Grandmother lived in the eighteen-eighties, had been destroyed in the 1953 floods. A previous farm they had near Goes is now covered in houses, but the hotel they ran in Zierikzee is still there, though now converted into flats. I have a photo showing my grandmother looking through an upstairs window, and another of her at the reins of a smart carriage.

The windmill of my grandfather's family in Haamstede is still operating to this day as a tourist attraction. A cousin over there sent me records of ancestors going back over five hundred years.

In contrast, I had only a couple of photos of my father's family in spite of him having twelve brothers and sisters. Most of them remain a mystery... although the family itself can, allegedly, be traced back to the Battle of Agincourt. Where we fought on the French side.

I have put together a series of stories detailing my adventures as I remembered them, and bring the story *almost* to the present. They sometimes involved fishing and were always ridiculous in some way.

Chapter 1: Wartime Streatham

Hitler was busy storming across Europe and coming ever closer to Jersey, where we were all living in 1940. It was just a matter of time before he reached the lightly defended Channel Islands. We left it a bit late but worries about our possible treatment by an invading army forced us on board one of the last ferries to mainland Britain.

Some thirty years after my two-year-old mother had fled across the channel with her parents… by a strange quirk of fate, I was two years old, and also fleeing across the channel. I was with the same group of people with the addition of my father and aunt. Some members of our group must have had a strange feeling of déjà vu.

My grandparents, with Aunt Jackie and Uncle Horace, went to the sleepy Kent town of Tenterden. Meanwhile, I travelled with my mother and father to Streatham, where my father had grown up and many of his family were still living. Father got a job working for his brother-in-law.

Being so young at the time, sadly I can provide no great anecdotes of our panic-stricken relocation, and I cannot remember my parents speaking of it. I believe they were bad times.

Hitler seemed intent on destroying London, using both incendiaries and high explosives—flying bombs, parachute mines, and finally rockets. Possibly every modern weapon then known to man. I was too immature to take it personally but was conscious of a great deal of noise.

Then we came to—to me—the most terrifying aspect of a world war, and something that has left scars on my very soul. Mother started to feed me boiled cabbage. Lunchtimes were a time of real terror that made even the ground shaking impact of a 500lb bomb pale into insignificance. (I shall mention cabbage again… and yet again and again in this book, dear reader. The vegetable was to become my bête noir.)

Mother must have been convinced by propaganda that I would not survive the war without it. Even after the war ended there was no escape.

I was taken to my first pantomime in Croydon and was "lucky" enough to be selected from the audience by a popular small celebrity at that time—Wee Georgie Wood. He dragged me from the safety of my seat to take the stage for a bubble blowing contest.

I lost the contest to an older girl by a very wide margin. I was devastated—beaten by a girl! However, for my pitiful effort, as if my public humiliation had already been enough, I was given a booby prize of… guess what?

A cabbage. "Just what we need for dinner," said my delighted mother.

The filthy vegetable went on to oppress me for my entire childhood. (Not that particular one obviously.) To make matters worse the whole garden seemed planted with them and I could see no salvation from the mealtime misery. I was sure Hitler must have dropped the seeds at the start of the war in an attempt to destroy our morale.

The garden in question was situated, in the traditional manner, behind our cottage which was one of six in Streatham High Road. These were originally built to house minions of the long-gone Coulthurst estate. Owned by William Coulthurst, of Coutts Bank.

Two solid brick-built cottages, possibly for a senior class of servant, were attached to four pokey, but picturesque, timber-fronted dwellings. Probably for scullions and stable hands.

We were lucky enough to have one of the brick ones—if lucky is the correct word. Although at that time anything with a roof, however basic, was a luxury. Many bombed-out families were dossing down with relatives, or in underground railway stations waiting for the council to rehouse them.

William Coulthurst had lived in the rather grand 'Streatham Lodge,' long pulled down and built over by that time. Only the servants' cottages remained and they were the sort of bijou residences which, if modernised, you would pay a great deal of money for today. I loved living there. Little boys don't need a lot of room, although they seem to take up a lot. It must have been hell for my mother. She had to manage with a small scullery equipped only with a gas cooker, a stone sink, and a coal-fired copper.

The copper always had to be fired up for laundry and bath-times. This involved carting coal about and ensuring there was always plenty of kindling wood. The bath itself resembled a galvanized coffin and usually hung on the wall outside the kitchen. The bath would just fit on the kitchen floor between the door and boiler, meaning coal had to be lifted across the bath, and anyone in it to keep the boiler stoked. A galvanized bucket was used to transfer hot water from boiler to bath... causing yet more hazardous situations in this limited space.

Bath nights were interesting to say the least, and needed family teamwork. However, I, while still small, could be stood in the kitchen sink and sponged down.

Gas lighting was an obvious boon when it first replaced candles and oil lamps. But only just. Compared to electricity it was horrible. The smell for a start. I remember being told that some fiend had added the smell deliberately to warn us of gas leaks, or things being left on while they were not alight. The smell actually crept past the flame, even after the device was lit, permeating the whole house and killing any flowers brought in from the garden.

Then there was the mantle. A small lacy piece of silk-like material fastened to a china ring. It would flare and balloon out slightly when lit for the first time. After that becoming so fragile you hardly dared even breathe on it. From that point it could last for years — *if* you could avoid touching it with the match when lighting it.

A princely rent of thirteen shillings a week was agreed for the cottage, and it was ours for the duration of the war, and longer if we should still be alive.

Father planted every food he could think of amongst the cabbage in the large back garden. Hitler was not going to starve us out. 'Dig for Victory!' we were told. Father even built an Anderson air raid shelter for us to hide in when the bombs dropped... Hitler was not going to win. We were British! At least, mostly.

The shelter soon became a rather damp and smelly hole in the ground, attracting all manner of garden vermin. It was an unpleasant place to frequent, but shelters like this kept many people alive as the blitz progressed. It certainly didn't do to be scared of spiders, or mice. On seeing a mouse, Mother would let out a blood-freezing scream that could even drown out the sound of an air-raid siren.

I remember us using the shelter a few times. It was a handy place for Mother to throw me when we had a surprise raid. Like most children I always wanted to stay out and see the bombs dropping and took exception to being taken by the scruff of the neck and thrown down a hole. An old mattress was put on the floor so no bones were broken. However, the Anderson shelter was no place to go when not faced with the gravest of dangers.

The communal shelter on the corner of Hilldown Road was then built by the authorities. It was only fifty yards from the front door and could provide us with more creature comforts. We much preferred it because it had tea making facilities, a primitive toilet and, best of all, human company.

It was reassuring to share the horrors of a night's bombing with other human beings rather than insects and rodents. Lifelong friendships were forged in such places as we cowered together and wondered if we would survive the night.

As well as the job with his brother-in-law's company, Father volunteered for the ARP (Air Raid Precautions.) Memories of Warden Hodges of Dads Army may spring to mind, but London was far removed from the fictitious Warminster-on-Sea. For the ARP in London, the reality was grimly different. Their number was made up mostly from building trade workers, and they were always first on the scene after—and even during—any air raid. They witnessed scenes that in the 21st century would guarantee a lifetime of counselling.

I remember Father telling me about ARP training, and being taught to use ladders to save people from the upper floors of buildings. When the bombs fell, all you needed was a shovel and a strong stomach.

I was fascinated by father's experiences while fire-watching in 1941. During one of the heaviest bombing raids he was on the roof of a high building somewhere in Streatham. In the distance, large parts of London were in flames as the bombs continuously rained down. It was like witnessing Hell... the bombers coming in wave after wave reducing the east of London to a huge firestorm no one could possibly survive... but survive they did.

On the radio in the room below him he could hear the eerie strains of 'English Country Garden' coming through the speaker. That moment was relived whenever he heard that tune for the rest of his life. I still think of him on that roof when I hear it.

After some months of digging out bodies and body parts he received his call-up papers. He was almost relieved as the carnage was starting to get to him. It continued to have a long-lasting effect on his nerves. With Father's departure, life became even more difficult for Mother with one lively three-year-old, another baby due, and trying to survive living in Victorian conditions among continual air raids.

There is one thing few people need to appreciate these days. Without a refrigerator it is necessary to go shopping several times a week. During the war this involved queuing outside shops, in all weathers, and having to sometimes dash for cover if the air-raid siren sounded.

The only way to lighten the burden for Mother, and at least secure safety for one of us, was to send me to my grandparents in Tenterden. It was a ridiculous situation. Mother's family had moved to England from Holland in 1910, when she was a two-year-old. Thirty years later, and married to an English serviceman, she was still a registered alien and not allowed into Kent—even though her parents and brother were living there. My aunt had been born after they moved to England, so she was British.

It was a restricted area. Invasion seemed likely and the authorities didn't like the idea of foreigners roaming around and possibly reporting back to the Germans. My grandparents were kept under close watch by the authorities and grandfather even had to obtain special permission to buy a bicycle.

Having been born here, I was also British, and as such, was able to duck out from the privations of life in London several times over the next few years to live with my aunt Jackie and grandparents in Tenterden.

Chapter 2: Tenterden and Other Wild Places

I was about three years old and my first memories date from this time. Some, naturally, are a little vague, but I have very vivid memories of my times in Tenterden as a toddler.

Grandfather had secured a position running a flower growing and market garden business in Tenterden. With this job came a nice house with a balcony, some rather sad tennis courts and a huge walled garden with greenhouses around the walls. It was at the bottom of a lane in the West Cross area of Tenterden.

Although trained as a flower grower my grandfather was passionate about growing tomatoes. His skills covered most aspects of farming. Growing flowers was not considered important during the war and he found himself growing anything that would feed the nation and help the war effort. Even potatoes. He probably grew cabbages somewhere, but, unlike my mother, my grandparents respected my culinary preferences and the possibility of my having tantrums at dinner times.

My grandmother was quite a character. A tall stout woman in her late fifties, she spoke a strange mixture of Dutch and English, sprinkled with the odd Welsh word she'd picked up while living in Wales in the 1920s. Many found her difficult to understand, but I soon cottoned on and started to use the odd Dutch word myself.

Dutch relatives visiting in the sixties and expecting to converse with her easily, found she still had the strong regional accent she had left Holland with, and found it easier to converse with her in English, in spite of the strange way she spoke it.

Grandfather spoke English well with only a slight accent. Having changed their surname to something the British could pronounce, he had also adopted the first name of Jack. He was a similar age to grandmother, around sixty at the outbreak of WWII. He was a good-looking man, of average height for the time, although he would be regarded as smallish these days. The family would rarely talk about what had caused them to come to England the first time, in nineteen-ten. When they did, they did so in hushed tones.

I always found grandfather kind and affable. He did spend time in the pub socializing, but I was never aware of any resulting drunkenness. He was well-educated, very hard-working and spoke several languages. During WW1 he had worked occasionally as an interpreter for a government department dealing with prisoners. Although he had many skills, including horse training, his most sought-after skill was still as a flower grower, and he was never without a decent job.

I didn't realize until many years later just how much my grandparents missed their families and their lives in Holland. They had photographs of every family member and suffered dreadful anxiety for them during Germany's occupation of Holland. Sadly, they lived out the rest of their lives in England, never returning to Zeeland.

As I grew old enough to know what was going on around me, life at West Cross Nurseries continued to be great fun for a youngster, with never a dull moment. I remember grandfather ploughing the small field running alongside the railway track. He had to wrestle with a two-wheeled tractor called an 'Iron Horse,' my first introduction to any sort of vehicle. You had to walk behind the thing to steer and it must have been like controlling a huge, motorised wheelbarrow with a plough attached. Although the nurseries had been allocated land army girls, none of them were able to use this particular beast. The dreadful state of the ground didn't help. At that time every scrap of space had to be used for food production. Once the 'Dig for Victory' campaign declined, no-one ever tried cultivating this particular strip of land again.

The railway that ran along the bottom of the field behind the house would in time become part of the Kent and East Sussex Railway. Local stories suggested it was so slow people would get out and pick flowers as it tried to make its way to the top of any slight incline. The trains often set fire to the bushes as they crawled slowly up the line between Rolvenden and Tenterden. Grandfather, and anyone else working nearby, would have to rush off and beat the flames out before they spread and did real damage.

At breaktime each day everyone would return to the house and drink Camp Coffee, a substitute for the real thing. It was made out of chicory and I loved Camp Coffee in hot milk. My grandfather always drank sweet tea without milk.

I remember being fascinated by a huge mound of cow dung in the walled garden. Isn't it strange how something so unpleasant can be so interesting to a small child? I tried to climb it of course, to the horror of the family. They were even more horrified when I led a rather immaculately dressed neighbour's child to the top of it and started chanting "I'm the King of the castle." I was strictly forbidden to go near it ever again.

The walled garden had other hazards that could provide unpleasant surprises for a small child. A vicious cockerel that lived there took to chasing me and pecking the backs of my legs. Until that time, I had never considered chickens a danger. The family found my encounters with the cockerel highly amusing, and clustered around the kitchen door to watch as though it were some Roman Gladiatorial contest… while at the same time making sure I wasn't getting hurt too much.

I tended to stay out of the walled garden after that unless there happened to be an adult with me, though encounters with birds were to become a recurring feature of my life.

Another early memory was watching the deadly dogfights being played out in the skies high above my little head when I was barely more than a toddler. The lack of imminent danger made them less frightening to my immature mind than the cockerel or cabbage.

In the summer of 1943, I returned to Streatham. I was then old enough to start school, it being high time I learned there were things other than war and travelling from place to place.

Mother enrolled me at Emmanuel Infant School, in Colmer Road. It was less than half a mile from where we lived, just a ten-minute walk for a child. In those days it was unthinkable for a boy to be taken to school by his mother as his credibility would be gone in an instant.

Mother would see me across the High Road outside our house so I could then safely toddle off to school without having to cross another main road. With the use of private cars having reduced to a trickle, main roads were not particularly dangerous in those days. Most vehicles with internal combustion engines were noisy and fairly infrequent. Trams were even noisier, but easily avoided.

However, Mother's worst fears were realized when a group of us found access to a couple of bomb-damaged houses on the route. These places were death traps and, looking back, it was surprising none of us were hurt. Chimneys and even entire rooms were on the point of collapse, and there were buildings like these in most streets. They made better playgrounds than any modern child can imagine and it was impossible to keep us out of them. Our parents drilled into us not to take away anything we found in the bombed-out houses or gardens… or we would be shot for looting.

Mother heard about our adventures of course, because all the mothers discussed what the children had been up to while queueing outside a shop somewhere. There was another infant school nearby that was also part of the Emmanuel Church franchise, so I was sent there instead.

It was in the opposite direction and the school faced Streatham Common. I remember little about it except there seemed to be a great deal of praying involved. There were no dangerous bombed buildings on the way to this school but it *was* alongside the PB Cow Rubber Factory, which was thought to be one of Hitler's prime targets. It somehow went the entire war without damage. Possibly because it was hidden in a residential area.

I remember the factory laying on a memorable Christmas party for the children, but otherwise little else about my time at the school. Come spring, it was time for me to get back to Tenterden.

There I was sent to the little school behind St Mildred's Church in the centre of the town. Talk in the playground was of incendiary bombs, conkers, and country pursuits. As a city boy I knew little about country pursuits but all about incendiary bombs, London being strewn with them. I also knew about the horrendous burns suffered by children who picked them up. Autumn saw me back in Streatham again.

I moved *finally* to a school in Streatham Vale, about a mile away. If I include the school in Tenterden it was my fourth infant school in about a year. I thought at the time that this one was the best school in the world. It was a sprawling collection of single storey buildings with centrally heated classrooms and a large playing field. It had a huge room full of toys to intrigue any new intake of infants who might have wanted to go home in the first couple of hours.

I remember our first proper lesson there. We were each given a sheet of paper, a pencil, a plywood cut-out of an animal… then told to draw around it.

We would spend playtimes collecting shrapnel from the field to prevent it from damaging the lawnmower's blades. A great deal of credit was attached to finding the largest piece.

Lessons, as with all schools at that time, were frequently interrupted by the air raid siren. When this happened, we walked briskly, in an orderly single file, to the shelters. We did everything in an orderly manner because we were British — at least that is what the teachers told us. We even marched in pairs from morning assembly while Miss Sydney played a suitable Schubert march on the piano.

My father was home on leave when the first doodlebug entered London. It was only a week or so after the D-Day landings and people had started to relax. We heard the familiar wail of the sirens followed by a sound like a flying motorcycle. Father turned the light out and lifted the blackout curtain to find out what was going on. Upon seeing the glow from the doodlebug's pulsejet engine, he said, "The cheeky sod's got his lights on." I remember it word for word because it was rare for my father to swear in the house.

In the following weeks all hell broke loose as flying bombs fell day and night. I never actually saw one in London, just heard them — the engine noise and then the bang.

I still recall the fear and tension in the Hilldown Road shelter. There was a point roughly above us where a great many of the doodlebug motors would cut out. They would then glide for a mile or so before hitting their planned target, usually the London docks and the East End.

I can remember a couple of times when the unthinkable happened and one cut out while still approaching us from the south. There was a communal sharp intake of breath… then uncanny silence, except for someone praying in hushed tones, and the odd stifled sob.

It might have been the effectiveness of prayer that ensured none fell closer than half a mile from us. Even then, the bang was ear-splitting as half a street was taken out. I have no doubt the people killed there had also prayed.

Mother went to the police station to check the possibilities of moving to Kent, in spite of her alien status, the invasion scares now being over.

"Even if they lock you up, you'll be safer than you are here," came the desk sergeant's unofficial response. A couple of days later I was in Tenterden again and it was like living inside some epic film.

I would watch the doodlebugs purposefully heading in a straight line for London. Only fighters and guns were able to stop them from inflicting death and destruction on the city.

The fighter planes seemed to float around them like butterflies, a dangerous dance as they tried desperately to bring them down with gunfire while remaining distant enough to avoid the resulting explosion damaging their aircraft. Some pilots even managed to touch wings to change the doodlebug's direction—an incredibly difficult feat due to the doodlebugs speed. They were faster than most of the fighters, until the Mosquito, Tempest, and jet-engined Gloucester Meteor were deployed. I was disappointed at being made to take cover when the action was nearby. The spent shells and cases spewing from the pursuing fighters had to fall somewhere and could easily kill a child, or even an adult.

After the action was over, I spent many hours trying to find the bullets and shell casings. I can't remember finding a single one.

A row of rabbit hutches on one side of the walled garden provided tasty meals but attracted rats and occasionally an inquisitive fox. We never did find out how it got in.

Although there was an unavoidable presence of death and destruction in those years. I was horrified by the bang and resulting death when grandfather shot one of the rats. He never did get the fox though. In spite of living through much of the Blitz in London it was the first time I had actually seen a gun discharged.

When my mother next came down to join us, she had my brother Adrian, now a toddler, with her. He somehow toddled into the tennis court, which had been relegated to a chicken run after the fox had helped itself to a couple of tasty dinners from the walled garden.

Adrian somehow managed to open the gate and get in… where he was viciously attacked by my old enemy, the cockerel. The creature clearly didn't like London children and finding a small defenceless one was more than he could have hoped for. But for my aunt's dexterity with a heavy stick, Adrian may have been killed or badly injured. I witnessed the whole episode from the lane alongside.

A heavy swipe from my aunt knocked the creature into the air… and while still airborne it received a slicing blow alongside the head. There was total silence among the hens as the dominant male staggered to its feet with its head to one side. The head stayed at a strange and comical angle. Then grandfather came on the scene and wrung its neck. A stern lesson to any fowl that should seek to attack a golden-haired toddler with powerful friends.

We had the damaged bird for Sunday dinner. A treat usually only available at Christmas, although everyone complained it was tough. I was just glad to see the back of the horrible thing.

In 1944 my grandparents bought a small farm at Reading Street, three miles away. For them and my uncle it was the start of a long gruelling grind to build greenhouses and turn it into a horticultural business.

Building materials were in short supply and bricks completely unobtainable. Plenty of cement could be had though, so the walls of the first greenhouses were built by hand-mixing and pouring it between two sheets of corrugated iron. This must have been backbreaking work but my grandfather and uncle somehow managed it between them.

I found out many years later it been built so well it was almost impossible to break up when the subsequent owners replaced the greenhouses.

The doodlebugs kept coming and were being shot down above our heads. I was now six and it was like a never-ending adventure. However, there was an interlude around this time, when Mother and the two of us children were evacuated to Monmouth. It was to be some months before I saw my grandparents again.

It was a long tiring journey by train, taking nearly two days. At some stations the WVS (Women's

Voluntary Service) were there with a welcome cup of tea, a sandwich and sometimes a piece of cake. We slept in the carriages, and hours were spent waiting on platforms for trains to take us on the next stage. It was another great adventure for me. Lost sleep and discomfort had become a way of life by then. Eventually we arrived in Monmouth, and it was a wondrous place, even having two rivers. We were billeted, along with two other families, in a huge rambling vicarage. The owner was unhappy at having us forced upon him but was always friendly towards us children.

There was much to intrigue a six-year-old. Convoys of American servicemen in lorries and tanks would pass on the road south. Along with Richard, who was the only other child close to my age staying at the vicarage, I would shout, "Got any gum, chum?" We were always rewarded with a shower of sweets and sugar lumps thrown to us by the servicemen, which we would proceed to fight over.

The vicarage had several outhouses. These were dark inside because they had no windows. We would dare each other to go into them, but I was never brave enough to go beyond the doorway. The fear of the unknown was still greater than the fear of high explosive.

There was a long foliage-covered garden wall that had a few plums growing on it. We would sometimes find one and then, of course, fight over it. Being a year younger than Richard, and noticeably smaller, I would always lose. I remember a stumpy little tree in the middle of the lawn. We climbed it only to find ourselves covered in earwigs.

Once again, my mother's worst fears were realized when we discovered the river. She had hoped we wouldn't find it, but we stumbled across it after spotting some railway signals on a distant hillside. All children seem to be magnetically drawn to a railway. I'm not sure what devilment we intended when we reached it, but we found our progress blocked by the river Wye. Far better than railway signals. Mother need not have worried though, because we had enough respect for the river not to take risks around it.

It seemed the sun always shone there. We were too far outside the town to go to school or maybe they didn't have room for us—we were never told. It was like living in paradise. Every day we would explore the riverbank and nearby woods.

We were becoming almost feral. Then like all good things it came to an end after only a few months. London, we were told, was safe enough for our return. So we said our farewells to paradise and after another long and uncomfortable train journey we were back in Streatham.

To my delight, the much-admired front garden of the cottage had become an overgrown jungle. I was quite disappointed when my mother cut the jungle down, dug the ground, and re-planted it with flowers. Women did that sort of thing then.

Father was demobbed a year after the war ended, and finding a better house was his first priority. For me it still seemed like a palace. I thought it quite nasty for people to have lavatories inside their houses.

I am not aware of the details, but my father entered some sort of agreement with the landlord, whereby if father would like to modernize the cottage, at his own expense, we could buy it for a nominal price when the landlord retired in a couple of years. These days such a deal would be considered reckless without reams of paper from solicitors but, as far as I know, it was a gentleman's agreement which the landlord would certainly have honoured. I believe there was a similar understanding with the tenant of the adjoining brick cottage, who my parents had fallen out with over something trivial.

The landlord had a rustic furniture business in a large shed adjacent to the cottages. He and his brother produced benches, garden arches and other rustic Godwottery. It was a great place to get sawdust for the cages of the various smelly pets I kept.

We had the electricity laid on just in time to buy a television for the Coronation. On the day our tiny dining room was packed with neighbours we had invited to watch it with us. Old Mrs Miller, who lived next door, refused to eat any of the sandwiches we provided. She said she couldn't possibly eat in front of the Queen. It would be so rude. Such strange things a child remembers.

Meanwhile, plans were being drawn up, and work started on the cottages. Modernization. Progress was slow only partly because of the cost, and mainly due to the dire shortage of materials. Father intended to do most of the work himself. Then it all came to a stop when the London County Council stepped in and decided the wooden fronted cottages, in spite of being picturesque and the last of old Streatham, came under their slum clearance scheme.

A compulsory purchase order was put on the whole site in 1954, including our two partly modernized brick-built dwellings, and the landlord's workshop. This was a shock because we thought slum clearance only involved East End tenements and battered dirty terraces.

There were petitions signed by hundreds of people to save this pretty and historic feature of old Streatham. My parents tried to get compensation for the money they'd already spent on modernization but were told their compensation would be a new council house. This turned out to be a prefab initially, then a flat on the second floor of a new block of flats… built on the site where our old house used to stand.

People were still used to being pushed about by the authorities. In wartime you just hadn't questioned things and accepted anything the faceless bureaucrats had demanded. Freedom from bureaucracy was still a few years off, and nothing was going to stop the council from bulldozing the site to erect an ugly block of flats. We were sorry to leave the little house in the High Road. For all of its being a bit primitive it had been warm and dry, and ultimately safe.

While living there I had also had my wonderful world in Tenterden to escape to every school holiday. I would board the coach at Victoria, change to a bus at Maidstone and Grandfather would collect me by car from Tenterden. I was then in the place I thought I belonged.

I spent much time walking the dog—a strange creature of indeterminate breed that only wanted to dig for rabbits. Returning from one outing I was in bad trouble for taking it through a field of sheep. The dog was on a lead but it was fairly large, and the farmer had doubts about a 'town boy' having the ability to control it. Care was taken to avoid the fellow's land after that.

My favourite activity was fishing in a dyke a few hundred yards from the Nurseries. I caught my first fish on rod and line from the bridge on the Appledore road… a total of three small perch. Grandmother fried them for my supper.

My grandparents kept a few pigs and there were smoked hams hung up around the oak beams. Breakfast consisted of thick slices of fatty bacon and fresh eggs from their own chickens. I have never been able to find bacon like that again. Unlike in the big towns, rationing was not so much a problem for country dwellers.

My grandparents were getting old and mother wanted to keep an eye on them so we finally moved down from London to Ashford, in 1957. They both died within a couple of years of each other in the early nineteen-sixties.

The nursery business at Reading Street passed out of the family when my uncle retired and has now evolved into a huge garden centre with a pleasant restaurant where we occasionally enjoy a meal. It occupies the piece of ground where I used to dig worms for fishing over seventy years ago.

Chapter 3: Wheels Without Engines

Wheels were to become a recurring feature of my life. My first set came early in my childhood. So early in fact, I cannot remember using them. They were attached to a large fluffy dog, along with a handle to support me in my first attempts to toddle on my hind legs.

I only became aware of the dog while chasing the first rat I had ever seen in our Streatham garden. The fluffy dog was in a sorry state, half-hidden under a sheet of corrugated iron, its filling of wood shavings scattered about where the rat had claimed squatter's rights. Something about the dog stirred a memory and I just knew it had once been a much-loved toy.

I was gripped by righteous indignation at the rat's behaviour and, bent on chastising the creature, seized a sharp stick I found lying amongst the junk. I had heard rats were nasty… Well, I could be nasty too. I poked violently at the wood shavings hanging out of the fluffy dog, forcing the rat to make an appearance. I stabbed it and whacked it with the sharp stick several times, until it passed out. Thinking it was dead I picked it up by the tail and ran indoors to show mother. The hunter-gatherer instinct was strong in one so young.

Mother's reaction to my catch was a surprise to me, not helped by the rat starting to regain consciousness and attempting to climb back up its tail and bite me.

It was an epic scream even by my mother's high standards, but she had been practicing it on mice for most of her life. The sight of a live rat being jiggled by the tail by her five-year-old son demanded that the scream had to be proportionally louder. I dropped the rat and clapped my hands to my ears. The rat staggered away into the kitchen to take refuge, becoming responsible for a nasty smell after expiring somewhere behind the copper.

I was not to be hailed as a conquering hero it seemed, and my first set of wheels found their way on to a bonfire.

A child's bicycle was a difficult thing to get hold of during WWII, but somehow my grandparents sourced one for me, while I was living with them a couple of years later. I remember being given it in the lane outside the house at West Cross. It looked like new but is unlikely to have been. The Norman Cycle works in Ashford, where it was manufactured, was on war work. It must have been in 1944, because we had not yet moved to the farm at Reading Street.

While sitting on the saddle, I could just reach the ground with the tips of my toes, which meant it would be useable for a couple of years as I grew taller. Still, it seemed a bit scary to ride. My aunt spent the next couple of hours running behind me up and down the lane... until I could balance properly, and no longer fell off. Luckily, a six-year old's cycle is pretty close to the ground and it was not far to fall, as I was to do then, and on many future occasions.

Later in the year I returned to London after a short spell of evacuation in Monmouth, (of which more later) to enjoy the possibility of the world peace

I had been told so much about. The bike was, eventually, to join me in London after the war really ended. However, not until I had used it on several school holidays in Tenterden and found out about punctures.

I find it difficult to believe I actually used to pedal the four miles from Reading Street to Tenterden. But I did, my little legs going up and down like pistons as I laboured up the steep hill that seemed to stretch for most of the journey. Normally I did not stop until the aptly named 'Rest a While' corner was reached at the little hamlet of Leigh Green.

On one such journey I found, upon reaching Tenterden, that I had one of these puncture things I had heard them talk about… the tyre had gone all soggy. Bicycle pumps were like gold dust at that time, and no one dared to leave one affixed to its bracket on their bike for fear of it being stolen. You always knew if someone had arrived by bike, because they would be carrying a pump.

Some kind person pumped up the tyre for me, but it was flat again before I had gone a mile on the way home… Fortunately, I was used to walking.

I could not wait to show the bike to my friends at school in Streatham, it was a quality machine and no one else had one made by Normans. In fact, bicycles were rare amongst children just after the war. This brought about the danger of it getting stolen, so my mother often met me halfway home from school, for what good that was likely to do.

The point came when the bike was far from immaculate and unlikely to be stolen. This point was reached in a remarkably short space of time, because I spent most of my life either on it, or picking myself up after falling off. Both the bike and myself shared a great deal of gravel rash.

One particular accident scarred me for life, (a small scar anyway). I was tearing down Arragon Gardens when I struck a patch of loose gravel. My front wheel slipped from beneath me and I was projected over the handlebars--where my face contacted the road and the gravel lubricated its progress for some way along it. Medical treatment was needed.

Only a matter of days after that one of my classmates had a fatal cycling accident on the way to school, and, on order of the headmaster, cycling to the establishment was banned for all of us.

When I became too big for it, the cycle passed on to my brother... who promptly had it stolen from the recreation ground. The attendant found and returned it to us a couple of weeks later, which was amazing... a small recreation ground actually having an attendant?

My uncle Bill was a small yet pugnacious man. He could have been a double for James Cagney. In spite of my father having a grand total of eleven siblings Uncle Bill was one of the few we ever saw.

A keen cyclist and employee of the Gas Board, Bill was a well-known character around that part of South Streatham and Norbury. He always had a tool bag and a length of gas pipe attached to the crossbar of his red Gas-board-issue bicycle. At weekends he would think nothing of cycling, on his own bike, a hundred miles in a day.

It was nearly time for me to upgrade to a small-adult size bicycle and, as luck would have it, one of Uncle Bill's cast-off cycles was available. It was not the sort of machine I would have chosen, as it did not have drop handlebars like a racing bike. However, it was well maintained, the brakes worked, and the straight handlebars were the next-best thing to dropped ones. I could not reach the ground with my toes unless I was alongside the curb, but I laughed at such hazards, putting at the back of my mind how far I now was from the ground.

I got on well with the bike and it served me well for a couple of years until I found something better — a machine resplendent with drop handlebars, gears, and a dynamo.

It was normal if you lived in a terraced house in those days, to have to negotiate several bicycles in the entrance hall. Living, as we and many other people did, on a main road, it was unwise to leave them outside. Padlocks were difficult to obtain for some time after the war, as were mother's nylon stockings, that kept getting snagged on the pedals as she tried to squeeze past. She used to make such a fuss over it.

However, I liked having wheels, and hoped to never be without them in some form or other.

Chapter 4: The Table

I must have first become aware of the table around the age of three or four. It was dark oak, three feet square, and had slightly chamfered Parsons-style legs. It also had a pull-out extension that made it a full five feet long for family banquets—rare occurrences in the wartime years.

All family meals were eaten at it, and it was privy to all our mealtime discussions. Father often came home to lunch when he was working locally and would put the world to rights and complain about his sister (who doubled as his employer's wife), and her right-wing politics.

My mother made occasional approving comments until it was her turn to tell who she had met shopping that morning, what had been said, and what had been bought.

The table became very well informed in the minutiae of our family's life.

One of the rare times we had the table extended to full length was when father acquired the makings of a table tennis set. The acquisition did not extend to a net, so books were balanced, spine up, across the table to make the game worth playing. We rummaged around until we came up with a strange selection of books that were approximately the right size. I remember using my school copy of the Bible—supplied generously by the Gideons in an attempt to show us little savages the ways of righteousness—a battered household management and ready reckoner with an Edwardian lady on the cover, and a copy of something called The Decameron. I found this relegated to a forgotten corner right at the back of the bookshelf.

The players developed a strange, stationary style through having to play in a foot-wide space at either end. This developed naturally as elbows smashed into the wall and new (to me) words were bandied about. There was something distinctly robotic about their movements. The game often ended with the celluloid ball bouncing into the fire and disappearing in a bright puff of flame.

I believe the table was originally a wedding present to my parents and was my mother's pride and joy. The details of style and utility were lost on me when I first encountered it, but I did quickly become familiar with the sharp corners of the table's top, my head regularly coming into contact with them.

The table lived in the cramped dining room in our cottage in Streatham High Road, along with a piano, a radio, and later on a television. It was the room where our family spent most of our time.

In those days, for most working-class families, the front room was sacrosanct, only used at Christmas and for special visitors. Or to lay out bodies if they happened to have any.

It did not make sense to me. I thought about it a lot while nursing my bruises. However, when I asked mother why we didn't use it when we were so cramped in the back room, she told me she was keeping it neat and tidy for when I got older and wanted to bring my girlfriends home. I was appalled. Nothing could have been further from my mind at that age than bringing a silly girl home. She would no doubt just sit and play with dolls. I concluded there must be some other reason they didn't want to tell me about.

As I grew taller the malevolent artefact graduated from giving me concussion to breaking my nose. Then splitting my lip and loosening my teeth. Mother always kept it highly polished and I began to associate the smell of furniture polish with the onset of serious pain. I was learning about pain and should have known by that time to avoid it, but I was a boisterous child and mother's warnings about running about in the house fell on deaf, as well as battered, ears.

At around six years old I grew too tall, or cautious, to suffer further injury. Father's threats to cut off the table's corners became less frequent. This was probably fortunate, as Mother pointed out, his carpentry skills going little further than his success in breaking up our piano with a sledgehammer. He little knew he was at the dawn of a sport that in later years would enjoy worldwide popularity.

The popularity of piano smashing reached its peak in the sixties, even spreading to America, where colleges would form 'Piano Reduction Study Groups'. With the advent of the gramophone, and later on radio, television, and the installation of jukeboxes in cafes, people no longer needed to make their own music. Old upright pianos were gathered together, and young hooligans were timed as they set about them with sledgehammers, breaking them down until all the pieces could be passed through a nine-inch hole. The winner would receive some sort of prize or accolade. Those were indeed dark times for culture and civilization.

The removal of our own piano gave us a little more room but cut short any ambitions my brother and I might have had of becoming concert pianists.

Returning to the table. I began to suspect it enjoyed divine protection in spite of its wickedness. Unlike the poor piano.

Less than two years later a familiar wail echoed through our humble abode, as my little brother's head, for the first time, contacted the corner of the table. By courtesy of the wartime priority milk and welfare orange juice, he had grown tall enough to carry on what was to become a family tradition. He exploited it to the full. He was noisier than I had been, because he was a sturdy little boy and had a stronger pair of lungs. The table settled in to enjoy another victim.

Fast-forward twenty-five years. My own children would return from a visit to their grandparents having sustained injuries that seemed strangely familiar.

On my parent's deaths I inherited the desirable heirloom and banished it to the corner of a spare room. Where, in harmless isolation, it could reflect on its shortcomings.

Eventually, my sons bought their own houses, and it was time to downsize. A vanload of surplus furniture went to the salerooms. But not the table. I couldn't let it go as it was part of my life, a link with my parents and my childhood in Streatham… besides, it knew too much.

My youngest son then became custodian of the wretched thing. Still solid and still with that brooding malevolence. I believe my grandson walked into it at some time. A third generation of our children hurt, in spite of having it in a decent sized room.

I sometimes wonder if the injuries inflicted blunted our intellects, rendering us all too dim to take an axe to the thing. Or had it just become smarter than us and was exerting some sort of control over our actions? It has gone now, and there is a shiny modern table where it once stood. My son has not mentioned what became of it, probably fearing I may have a deep-seated sentimental attachment to the thing.

In the times of darkness and insecurity suffered by the old in the early hours of the morning I sometimes remember the table and wonder where it is. Usually when I have been laying awkwardly on one of my ears.

Chapter 5: The Parrot Who Taught Father to Swear

When we first moved to Streatham a parrot lived next door. It was reputed to be an Amazon Green. I knew this to be right because of its colour, sinister foreign accent, and evil disposition. Another entry in the list of birds to add interest, or pain, to my life

It was the companion of a very old sea captain's widow, who fed it and did odd jobs around the house for it. It was a strange quirky creature; the parrot that is. Someone with great imagination had given it the name of Polly. The old seafarer's widow was known as Mrs Corcoran.

I liked parrots. They reminded me of Long John Silver in Treasure Island and other sorts of raffish and piratical folk. I had recently read Treasure Island and my mind was full of it. I was sure Polly knew where some treasure was buried, and that if I could only teach it to say, "Pieces of eight." I would be on my way to a fortune. However, getting close to it was fraught with danger.

Sadly, when parrots and old ladies team up together it's easy to predict which will fall off the perch first. In 1946 the inevitable happened. Mrs Corcoran did not return from hospital. My mother had foolishly expressed interest in the creature at some time or other, and offered to feed it while Mrs Corcoran was in hospital. It was suddenly ours.

An ornate cage appeared in our living room surrounded by seed husks and menace. Another beak to feed. Polly didn't like men. In fact, she detested them. Whether this dislike went back to its days before the mast having to spend uncomfortable years on the shoulder of a man with dirty ears, we will never know.

Polly used bad words. Very bad words. If I ever repeated any of them in the house it earned me a light tap around the ear from my father. I noted that he didn't try tapping the parrot round the ear when it said the same thing.

The bird adored my mother, who consequently won the job of feeding and cleaning out the brute. My father and I steered clear, aware that it was out to get us if it had half a chance. There was something about the way the creature looked at men that froze the blood.

One day, while mother was out shopping, Polly made a reasonable request for some 'Effing seed,' adding a few more expletives to underline the urgency of its request. The horrible thing had knocked its seed dish to the floor of its cage in a fit of pique and try as I might, I couldn't re-fill it through the safe aperture provided. I went to father repeating the parrot's request, ducking as I did so, and explained the problem with the seed tray.

All father did was to express apathy, and the wish that the rotten creature might starve and all its feathers drop out. Or something along those lines. The parrot must have heard what he said because the subsequent abuse from the hungry bird reached such a crescendo, we feared the police might be called.

Father girded his loins. At the time I was not entirely sure what that meant but I had heard the words used in similar circumstances. He bravely thrust his hand into the cage, hoping to return the dish to its rightful place before the parrot noticed him.

Polly looked at him, its head turned to one side in a quizzical, monocular sort of way, which suggested menace and evil intent at the same time. As the hand came within its reach the creature moved like lightning. There was a howl as Father withdrew his hand from the cage with Polly clinging, by claws and beak, to the back.

Father then used words I recognized from the parrot's repertoire, continuing to embellish them until the bird released him, hopped on to the mantlepiece and defecated loudly. There it sat, defying anyone to go near it until Mother returned from shopping.

With her arrival its demeanour changed completely. It looked at her adoringly and croaked "Who's a pretty boy then?" as if butter wouldn't melt in its beak. Mother held out her hand. It hopped on to it and was returned to its cage.

Upon regaining the safety of its perch, Polly, in a leisurely fashion, started to wipe the blood from its beak with a look of triumph in its horrid beady little eyes.

"I hope you've not been tormenting the poor creature," Mother said sternly as Father held out a ravaged hand for inspection.

Having spent the previous four years fighting Hitler, Father was justifiably upset by Mother's lack of sympathy; also, at being, "Beaten up in my own home by a bloody parrot," as he put it.

For the next few weeks, the parrot strutted about its perch with a self-satisfied look about its beak, unaware that plans were afoot for its banishment. Polly had to go because there were fears for my little brother's safety. A cockerel had already tried to eat him, and for all we knew his flesh might have been irresistible to all types of fowl. We were promised a nice harmless little budgie to replace it.

Polly had worked hard ingratiating itself with mother, and she had a sneaking regard for it, but with the rest of the family exerting pressure she eventually found another elderly neighbour who was willing to give the creature such sanctuary as it may need. The old lady claimed to be immune to foul language, having once carried the Salvation Army collection box around East End pubs. Furthermore, she was certain that with 'Divine help,' she would rid the bird of the devil's influence. The words were hardly out of her mouth before the malevolent avian was in her lounge, with a complimentary box of seed and the good wishes of our entire family.

There were tears from my mother, both as the cage went out of the door and later when visiting the pet shop to buy a budgie. The pet shop owner asked why she was no longer buying seed for the parrot, jokingly telling her a budgie would be no substitute for seed and would not give the parrot a balanced diet. When told we had given the bird away and the budgie was a replacement for it, he expressed regret and told her he would have given at least five pounds for the bird and cage. A useful amount of money in 1946.

I learned some years later that an Amazon green parrot can live for over sixty years if kept fuelled up with the right sort of seed. Is it possible it outlived my parents? It certainly won't outlive me though.

Chapter 6: Of Ducks and Things.

At junior school in the 1940s names were pretty ordinary, mostly biblical or from kings and other famous people. I soon found out that I was the only boy by the name of Donald and, as far as I know, none of the girls had the name either. There were only two Donalds that existed in the world of schoolchildren in those days. One was a famous cricketer, named Don Bradman, the other a quarrelsome Disney cartoon duck.

There is no doubt whatsoever that the duck was the most famous of the two but the children of our school should have considered themselves fortunate. Because they also had *me*.

They could have nicknamed me Bradman and I wouldn't have minded. He was after all a famous and courageous batsman, even though he was Australian. However, children are cruel and like the occasional laugh, so I was called… Quack! Once again, a bird was making my life difficult. Firstly, the vicious cockerel, then that dreadful parrot… and now ducks.

For a while it seemed that there were ducks quacking behind my back wherever I went in the playground. In the classroom, soft quacking noises sometimes emanated from the back seats. This became slightly less frequent as I caught and physically reprimanded several of the 'Quackers'—mainly the ones who were not too big. As a result, I became quite a scrapper in my early school days. It was ironic, however, that no one actually called me Donald.

Although it *was* my name, I was always known as Tony. This avoided confusion with my father who was, for some reason I had yet to understand, also named Donald.

I dreaded that rollcall by the teacher each morning, knowing that it would expose my real name to all and sundry, and provoke a quiet quack from one of the back seats. I tried to identify the culprit, or culprits, but there was always some doubt. Even the teacher couldn't spot them. Thankfully, the teacher cottoned on after a while and began to also call me Tony, even in the rollcall.

The quacking noises and resulting fights became fewer, and in almost a matter of weeks were forgotten. But the scars on my psyche remained.

Ducks were to rear their ugly beaks once more in my young life when mother confessed to a liking for duck eggs—virtually unobtainable at that time in post-war London. A roll of chicken wire appeared in the garden followed by some frantic hammer wielding and occasional swearing by my father.

He had just been demobbed after having to hang around doing nothing in the army for months after the war ended. He was desperate to find something to do before starting his new job. It has been mentioned before that although having trained in the building trade he was no carpenter by any stretch of the imagination. A crude compound for ducks was knocked together from odd pieces of timber that could have more beneficially been used as kindling to light the fire. Mercifully, the ducks were never to catch sight of it. I remember the ducklings being collected in a box from Mayday Road, in

Croydon, and I was fascinated by dozens of day-old chicks in the window.

My parents had bought day-old chicks in the past. The smelly little blighters had been corralled in a shallow box alongside the hearth in our cramped living room. Seemingly for weeks. Eventually the survivors were considered old enough to go outside and die there instead. Sometimes a couple would survive. Otherwise it would mean buying 'point of lay hens.' An altogether more expensive proposition, but one that saves a great deal of guano and dead body disposal. To say nothing of whiffy little pests running around indoors.

Watching the endearing little bundles of fluff chirruping and skipping about in the box by the fireside, I was blissfully unaware, at that time, of other, less humane, uses for them in zoos and laboratories.

Where the ducklings were concerned the story was even worse than the chicks. They were corralled alongside the fire in the lounge, where they became unwell. At least, my mother *thought* they looked unwell. I had no idea what was wrong with them, except that they smelled even more foul than the day-old chicks. Halitosis maybe?

While mother was very experienced with chickens, often having revived them with a spoonful of cod liver oil forced between their beaks before they died, she knew little about ducks. But it seemed logical to her that a medicine suitable for children and chickens, should also be beneficial to ducks.

She forced some cod liver oil between their reluctant bills, and they were all dead by morning.

The production of duck eggs was no longer considered viable. In any case, the suitability of our garden for waterfowl was questionable, because the only water available was an inch or so, in an upturned dustbin lid. I had thought the dustbin lid a good place to keep tadpoles until they eventually turned into frogs and benefitted the garden. I had captured the little fellows during an expedition to the deepest, darkest reaches of Mitcham Common Swamps.

This was a place where many feared to tread, and one was guaranteed to return from this mangrove-like area with wet and muddy shoes and socks. A sartorial hallmark I was fated to carry with me for most of my childhood.

Gazing, with interest, from their jam-jar, the tadpoles endured a fourpenny bus-ride and a fascinating walk down Streatham High Road where all of life was on view. This was a world rarely seen by baby batrachians. I like to think the experience enhanced their lives to some extent before I let them loose in their sunny, interesting, and comfortable pool. I had even brought back some pondweed, and chucked in a half-brick and some stones to add sophistication as well as something to hide behind.

There was bright sunshine the day after they moved in and they were all boiled alive in the shallow, unshaded water. A passing blackbird was delighted to pick their bodies out of the water, accepting the gourmet offering of Boiled Tadpole as something it rarely saw on the menu. But I digress. Enough about amphibians… back to ducks.

Whenever fishing, or even walking past a village pond, in the following years I seemed to invite a derisory 'quack' from somewhere in every clump of reeds. I knew they could see me, but I couldn't see them. There was something disturbing about this.

It was many years later while looking at a Gary Larson cartoon book I discovered what my problem was. Anatidaephobia. The fear that somehow, somewhere, a duck is watching you.

Chapter 7: Golden Eagle

The Golden Eagle in question was, surprisingly given my peculiar affinity with avians, not the bird but a boat. Boats were another entity to feature prominently in my life and this was my first experience of one.

Shortly after the war ended, paddle steamers resumed their pleasure cruises from London Tower Bridge. The local cockneys could now regain their sea-legs and steam down the horribly polluted Thames as far as Margate with paddles chunkin' as in Kipling's 'Road to Mandalay' — a poem every Englishman knew by heart at that time.

The Royal Eagle was a ship for the officers and toffs. It boasted high dining, champagne, and comfortable lounges. Being cleverly marketed as 'London's Own Luxury Liner' it cost a full eight shillings a head to cruise from London to Margate.

Then there was the Crested Eagle, known as the 'Greyhound of the River'. From Tower Bridge, it dashed up the east coast to Clacton, having to maintain a speed of at least 13 knots in order to visit some ten piers. Passengers even a minute late back to the ship had to go home by train. All too manic for the likes of us.

Then there was the Golden Eagle, for the hoi-polloi. All together more laid-back with its vomit-resistant decking, fish and chips, and pork pies. One could get drunk on bottles of brown or light ale, and it had slatted, easily hosed-down seats to sit on in the deck area. It was marketed as 'The Happy Ship', and only cost four shillings a head. Possibly less if you were only going as far as Southend. Our family booked a trip to Southend on the Golden Eagle in the summer of 1947.

Mum, Dad, little brother, and I caught a bus from landlocked Streatham to Tower Bridge. There we boarded our first ship, eager for a taste of the seafaring life. As the brown ale started to flow the happy ship reputation began to make itself felt—lots of laughter and good fellowship. Then our own version of fine dining—corned beef sandwiches, bags of crisps, and a vacuum flask of tea laid out on the slatted seats.

We had a running commentary over the Tannoy system, identifying all the points of historical and other interest along both banks. I particularly remember passing the OXO factory and the commentator, a bit of a wag, remarking it was the only place you could get a square meal for a ha'penny. The groans and uproarious laughter went over my head and Father had to explain the joke.

Later on, as we passed their loading point at Becton, the commentator declined to mention the famous 'Becton Bovril Boats', the intrepid boats and crew that transported vast amounts of sewage for dumping just outside the estuary. Father took great relish in telling me about it, causing my imagination to work overtime but doing little for my appetite.

It was misty when we arrived at Southend, and I was confused. It appeared they were unloading us into a shed on stilts surrounded by sea. We then had a train journey down the pier and the town appeared gradually out of the mist in all its glory. This was where the fun was meant to begin for us kids.

Swimming trunks and tin buckets and spades appeared from a large bag Father had been carrying. Thus equipped, and wearing swimming costumes, we were let loose on a vast expanse of mud and shingle. It was time for Mother and Father to overdose on cockles and brown shrimps. They looked ghastly to children who had never seen them before.

I liked mud and it continued to feature prominently throughout my childhood. I just couldn't avoid the stuff and here in Southend there was more of it then I ever thought existed. We found pools containing little crabs and our first lesson about sea life. Some of it was spiteful. Even small crabs can pinch painfully. We had yet to experience jellyfish to realize how bad it could be.

Filling our buckets with reluctant crabs, having learned the safest way of picking them up, we let them loose inside our mud castle. The tide eventually came in from somewhere and swept it all away, hopefully soothing the jangled nerves of the now thoroughly traumatized little critters.

The water looked dirty, but nevertheless we plunged in because that was what the seaside was for. We had seen pictures of it. It was too shallow to swim which I found disappointing, the water only coming up to our waists if we sat down.

"You have to wait until the tide is fully in," Father told us.

Splashing about in the shallows something slimy brushed my leg. 'Octopus!' I thought, and jumped a couple of feet. Then I looked down and saw how dirty the water really was. We were literally paddling in sewage. We found a fresh water tap near the promenade and scrubbed ourselves.

Southend was ruined for us and my parents were hoping the cockles and shrimps they had just eaten were not local.

The trip home was noisy, though there was no more commentary over the Tannoy. "Someone probably slung the chap overboard," Father said. There was just popular music as the Golden Eagle sailed back up the Thames, packed with people determined to enjoy themselves. Fish and chips were bought and enjoyed. There seemed something quite nice about eating fish and chips on the deck of a boat. Us kids washed it down with lemonade, my father, unusually, with a bottle of light ale, while Mother was treated to port and lemon.

"I signed the pledge as a youngster," Father was always telling me. I was to wonder what that meant for a long time. Finding out eventually it was something to do with *his* father, a hydraulic engineer, drinking away a fortune, and carelessly leaving his leg under a Croydon-bound tramcar. I never knew my paternal grandfather and he was never talked about.

Strangely enough, the hit song of the moment was 'Cruising Down the River'. Everyone was singing it and they played it at least four times over the Tannoy. As things further deteriorated, I had my first sight of the strange rituals of Cockneys at play. They cleared part of the deck and were dancing to things called: 'Knees up Mother Brown', 'The Hokey-Cokey', and 'Lambeth Walk'. I thought it a grisly thing for children to see old people capering about in this way and if anyone had told me I would be doing these dances myself ten years later in the Streatham Locarno Ballroom, I would never have believed them.

There were empty bottles and fish and chip wrappings everywhere, to say nothing of the crisp packets and cigarette ends. It was a bit like a bloodless battlefield. I noticed a great deal of staggering, saw several people being sick and wondered why. I had never seen drunkenness but had heard of seasickness.

"Seasickness. It can be worse in calm weather," Father told me, when I pointed out the river was dead calm, yet people were being sick. Another thing learned that I thought might serve me well in later life.

We fell asleep on the bus home. It had been, in all, a smashing day out. It was to be over twenty-five years before I went to Southend again, by car. The sea looked a bit cleaner and, for an adult, it seemed quite a fun place. I even ate some cockles.

I was reminded of our Golden Eagle adventure many years later, when a friend told me stories about working aboard one of the 'Becton Bovril boats'. On one trip an unusual discrepancy in water depth was spotted on the echo sounder as they approached the Thames Barrier. It turned out the boat was riding low in the water because they had forgotten to jettison the cargo.

I can't help wondering how often that had happened in the past... and where they dumped it!

Chapter 8: Greatstone

Two years after the war ended, we had our first seaside holiday. Grandfather had arranged some accommodation for two weeks in New Romney, fairly close to the sea. There was much to plan. It was not just a matter of loading the car and setting off in those days.

A family holiday away was to be a great expression of freedom after six years of war... of being told what we could and couldn't do. There was a great deal of organizing required though, and many people had forgotten how to do it.

Things were still rationed and some completely unobtainable, which is why one of the new holiday camps would have been a good option. They were rumoured to have plenty of food available for campers. However, at that time they were something of an unknown quantity and the butt of music hall jokes about them being run to a strict military regime. Apparently, some of them had been used as military camps during the war, and the strict regime ethos may have entered the very fabric of the places.

My family liked to do things our own way, so such things were not for us.

One thing we could rely on was the public transport. The railways in particular, before the dreadful Doctor Beeching vandalism, could take you within a few miles of any place you wanted to go. Usually on time.

In those days our family was always faced with one problem when we wanted to go away—our three chickens. These little feathery egg machines were still essential if we wanted a regular supply of eggs, and they were part of the family. I don't remember their names after all this time, but I'm sure they won't mind me referring to them as 'The Chickens.'

Since the last few years of the war, we had taken to keeping them in our back garden and they had actually survived from day-old chicks... many hadn't as I may have explained in a previous chapter. My mother with her farming background knew all about such things and under her supervision, the little darlings gave us a regular supply of eggs.

We also became the local experts in the black arts of chicken keeping. At one time Father became Lord High Executioner of chickens, with me acting as his assistant and comforter of the remaining fowl should they be distressed by events. They never were.

It was fairly easy to teach townies to keep poultry, but when it came to dispatching them men who had returned from the war with dozens of enemy deaths to their credit, backed away in fear at the thought killing a single bird—even for Christmas dinner.

I wondered, in later years, if the Battle of Britain might well have gone the other way had Hitler sent over a flock of Rhode Island Reds, rather than Heinkel's and Messerschmitt's.

My job as executioner's assistant came to an end when the head came off one of Mrs Gray's chickens while its neck was being wrung. Father dropped it, and it ran away up the garden path without a head. This made me feel a bit icky so I chose not to attend any more executions.

Back to our own chickens' welfare though, and the problem that presented. The old lady next door had kept an eye on them a couple of times, but it was now getting too much for her. There had been a fatality the last time, with a chicken becoming trapped between the coop and the fence. By the time it was found it was long dead and it had to be hurriedly buried in the garden to get rid of the smell. As a fertilizer the dead chicken proved excellent... but we had not only lost a good source of eggs, but also a possible Christmas dinner.

With no one being available to help the only answer was to take the chickens with us. They deserved a holiday.

At that time, we only had the three Rhode Island Reds. All excellent egg layers and we had been told the breed travelled well. We found them a spacious box, and holes were drilled in the top and sides for them to breathe. The poor creatures, despite their apprehensive body language, were sealed in for the journey.

This box had to be carried as far the tram stop with all the other luggage and Father was only just able to manage it. He no doubt wondered if it would have been better made out of cardboard than wood. We all had to carry something. Even little Adrian carried a box that probably contained father's holiday hoard of Woodbine cigarettes. Our family's Sherpa-like progress, as we filed out on to Streatham High Road to board a number 16 tram, must have resembled a classic assault on Everest.

Once our train arrived at Norbury station, Mother gave careful instructions to the guard regarding the requirements of a trio of Rhode Island Reds who fate had decreed should travel south, in a box. The chicken's mystery tour then continued in the guard's van until we reached Redhill. There we transhipped to a train bound for Headcorn, where a final train took us to Tenterden. The worst part of the journey was now over. Grandad collected us by car from the station and took us on to Tollgate Nurseries.

The well-travelled and deeply apprehensive chickens were then released amongst the locals, who, as a welcome, gave them a good beaking over leaving little doubt as to the pecking order.

It was a strange, painful, and worrying place for our much-loved chickens to find themselves, but the irrepressible good humour of the average Cockney hen was bound to win through in the end. At least they had plenty of room to run around. This proved useful in view of the natives' hostility.

Leaving the chickens to their fate, Grandfather took us to our luxurious holiday accommodation. It turned out to be a caravan in a field on the outskirts of New Romney. It was surrounded by grass nearly two-foot high. However, on the plus side, we were delighted to find ourselves alongside the RHDR Railway. At this time the whole fleet of 15" gauge trains were being recommissioned following their wartime duties.

The caravan was modern for those times but very basic by today's standards. It had spiteful and intrusive springs in the beds, and minimal cooking facilities. The toilet was down at the local pub.

However, our family were used to journeying to distant toilets and our bladders had evolved accordingly.

Each morning, after Mother had fought for about an hour with a spirit stove to make a breakfast — which always tasted heavenly — we would wander down a long straight lane to the beach at Littlestone. Sometimes we went another half-mile to the sand dunes at Greatstone. The air was clean and fresh, and the white painted houses a pleasant change from the bomb-damaged and smoke-blackened buildings back in London.

Once at Greatstone Adrian and I had a feeling of freedom. We threw ourselves off the higher dunes and rolled down the slopes. We had only ever seen sand dunes in pictures, and that had been in the desert littered with tanks and artillery. That should have been a warning to us. Some barbed wire from the wartime defences still remained buried in the Greatstone dunes, and a couple of nasty cuts were collected.

Near to the dunes was a baker's shop selling coconut pyramids. We knew of nowhere else these could be bought, even in Streatham. They became a much-anticipated holiday treat each time we returned there over the next five years.

After a fabulous fortnight, that even my parents enjoyed, the holiday ended and Grandfather picked us up from New Romney.

The chickens had to be caught and boxed for the journey home. They had made good use of the extra space during their sojourn at Tollgate Nurseries, becoming quite athletic and difficult to catch. Having eventually made friends with the locals I think they were sorry to leave the wide-open spaces and return to their little wire compound in south London. They would have been sorrier still if the poor devils had known what was in store for them during the journey.

It had developed into a sweltering hot day and when we changed trains at Redhill we found the chickens had been buried under other luggage in the guard's van. The poor creatures were on their last legs. Mother was quite abrupt with the guard responsible. The semi-conscious fowl were removed from the box and a sad little tableau, of a sort rarely seen on Southern Railways' property, was enacted there in the middle of platform three. A porter found a bucket of water and the poor chickens had their heads dunked in it in the hope of reviving them. The whole thing resembled some sort of bizarre christening.

Many people gathered around to offer advice, but we were handling a situation rare in most people's experience. One of chickens didn't make it. Whether as a result of the original suffocation, drowning from being over-enthusiastically baptised, or just being tired of life and the continual surprises it brings we will never know, but our return to Streatham was tinged with a sadness that even a chicken dinner did little to lessen.

Greatstone became another of the dream places to feed my imagination during term time and grey days. Up to the end of the forties and on in to the fifties we would enjoy holidays in Greatstone. I found a place where I could hire a bicycle, and was able go fishing in a lake near Dungeness.

We harvested cockles at low tide at Littlestone, finding them with our toes while paddling about in the mud. We found that cockles, freshly boiled, bore no resemblance to the salty pieces of gristle sold by a seafood stall. We just tossed them in some butter, sprinkled on some pepper and ate them still warm.

Trips to Hythe, and later to Dungeness, in the little train became an important part of our summer. Even the last of the wartime barbed wire was disappearing from the sand, making an extensive medical kit no longer a necessity.

My last stay there was in 1955. I rode there on a motorcycle and camped amongst the dunes with my cousins. The stay was memorable.

There were incredibly high winds, forcing me to attempt cooking my breakfast inside the tent. This was not wise.

Cooking was still a mystery to me. I had much to learn and one of the lessons was that you can't fry everything, as I found out when I poured some baked beans in to the pan alongside the sausages and bacon. The pan caught fire and I found myself trapped in an inferno.

The tent doors were tied together, but fortunately it was pegged down in soft sand. I managed to somersault out of it with my eyebrows badly singed, then quickly fold it up and bury it in the sand to stop it smouldering. Breakfast was ruined and I was left standing forlornly amongst the swirling sand of the dunes, lacking cover and sustenance.

The wind was so strong the trip had to be abandoned. After an epic journey in the gale we somehow got back to Tollgate Nurseries. Quite an achievement on a motorbike, but even more so for my cousins on bicycles. Once there, the wind became so bad it blew out a greenhouse and sheets of glass sliced horizontally across the road. Fortunately, no one was injured.

Chapter 9: Beetles

It was 1947. The war had been over for two years but we still had rationing, and many things were in short supply.

Small children stalked the streets and bombsites bent on devilry. Few people realized this until there were reports of them being dug, in a sorry state, from a bomb-damaged house or dredged from a static water tank. The children of London were suffering from an acute bout of anti-climax in spite of the world resembling an adventure playground.

They told us everything would be different when the war was over, but it wasn't. It was more boring and they hadn't even displayed Hitler's head on a pole as the adults had promised. We just didn't know where we were going.

Keith was my first real friend at school. He lived in Ellison Road, halfway between my house and the school. He and I were looking for some sort for adventure as we looked through the railings of the bridge crossing the Graveney in the short lane leading to Runnemede Crescent. It was early October, and the evenings were getting dark so there would be no running wild in Streatham Common woods. "And bet your life something boring will be on the radio," I lamented.

Keith gazed through the railings and along the culvert where the river Graveney flowed. We could almost see it emerging from Beetles Bridge in the distance. Keith was deep in thought. "You ever been under Beetles Bridge?" he asked.

I had seen Beetles Bridge close up. It was alongside my Uncle Arthur's builder's yard and looked scary. The story had been spread amongst the local children that huge beetles lurked there, with pincers, shiny wings, and a spiteful disposition.

"I don't really like beetles," I told Keith. "At least, not the very big ones. How big are the ones in there?"

"I saw one this big once," he exaggerated, holding his hands about six inches apart, "with huge pincers."

The temptation to see such a creature—from a safe distance of course—was too much. I agreed to join him in a quick reconnaissance of the bridge entrance.

The Graveney could become a raging torrent when it rained heavily upstream. The water built up in Norbury Brook until, with loud roar, a tidal wave bore down the culvert sweeping all before it. That's what we had been told. The reality was not quite that dramatic. But that day the water was low. The sky suggested no tidal wave was imminent. We squeezed through a loose railing in the alleyway and lowered ourselves into the culvert.

It was the second time I had been down there that year and I was mindful of the trouble I had got into the previous time. The river had been only a few inches deep but flowing quite fast. In the interest of experimentation and knowing how things, like wellingtons, worked I had decided I should take my new ones for a test flight. After all, the worst thing that could happen was some water splash over the top.

I had lowered myself from the railings until one wellington contacted the water. There was a slurping sound and a pull on my leg as if some monster had grabbed my foot. I yelled in terror as, to my horror, the wellington was dragged from my leg by the current and bobbed off downstream, never to be seen again. Only by clinging desperately to the railing did I avoid following it. I had hopped the rest of the way home from school wearing only one boot.

Children's wellingtons were hard to come by and very expensive in that post-war period. I got into more trouble than I could ever have imagined and was still serving time on parental probation.

However, I wasn't wearing wellingtons on that particular day. The river was down to a two-foot-wide trickle, leaving an eighteen-inch space between it and the wall of the culvert. This was ample room for a couple of small boys to trot the hundred yards or so to the entrance of Beetles Bridge

On arriving at the bridge, we looked nervously inside. There was a shadowy sort of darkness that could have concealed anything, but at least we could see the light at the other end.

"After you," said Keith.

"Not likely! It was your idea," I told him.

We cautiously entered the dark and smelly tunnel. Ten yards ahead there was a movement.

"Beetle," screamed Keith in terror.

At that same time a train that had been lurking in Norbury Railway station passed over the bridge. The noise amplified in the tunnel to become an ear-splitting roar.

"Tidal wave," I shouted, and we fled.

Once out of the tunnel and running as fast as I could, I looked back to make sure Keith was okay, but taking my eyes off the culvert ahead. I trod on the slime where the outflow from one of the street drains emptied into the culvert. I landed heavily on my backside. Then slid down the slick of algae into the centre of the river.

It was only four inches deep, and half an inch of that was thick green slime. Keith helped me out and I hobbled behind him towards safety, no longer fearful of beetles or tidal waves.

Back at the loose railing we climbed out into the alleyway. I was not looking my best, with a slimy green stripe running up my leg and across the seat of my trousers. We discussed the beetle Keith had seen and concluded it was probably a rat.

"What a waste of an adventure," I said, fearing what my parents would say when they found out I'd been in the river again. The green slime covering my trousers was sure to give the game away. For some reason my father found my explanation of the Beetles Bridge adventure hilarious.

Mother was tight-lipped and furious at having to wash the green slime off my clothes. It was she that had the unpleasant task stoking up the kitchen boiler. Washing clothes was no fun in a Victorian house with no electricity. A washing machine was not an option in those days, even with electricity… unless you were very rich.

Little did any of us know that to come home with dirty or ruined clothes was to become a regular habit for both me and my little brother throughout our childhood. Fate had somehow decreed it.

"These beetles? Under the bridge you say?" Father asked.

"Yes, that's why it's called Beetles Bridge," I said smugly, feeling torn between happiness that I knew something Father didn't, but also wishing he would forget about the whole business.

"Did you know the bridge is named after the people who own the land around it?" he asked me. Such a boring piece of information was of no consequence to me, but I thought it wise to show interest.

"I grew up in Colmer Road, just yards away from the bridge. I used to play there as a child myself," he said, barely able to supress his laughter. "The landowner's name used to be Beadle, and it's actually known as Beadle's Bridge. Nothing to do with beetles."

This time *both* my parents burst into laughter.

Chapter 10: Delinquents

In the early post-war days, marbles were valued above rubies by small boys. Playing marbles was popular, but due to supply problems we used only two of them. The proper game involved loads, but we couldn't think of anyone in post-war history ever owning that many marbles.

"I've got hundreds of marbles at home," the upper-form rich-girl said. We knew Rachel was rich because she had told us so, and her claim was enhanced by her being well dressed and chubby. Chubby children were rare unless they had been stealing pies.

Hundreds of marbles though? No-one was that rich. We laughed and told her to prove it. True to her word she turned up the following day with a draw-string bag containing dozens and dozens of shiny, brand new, marbles. She stood in the playground and as we filed past, she gave each of us a tantalizing glimpse of what it is like to be rich as she opened and closed the bag. With Rachel being so rich, it went without saying she would share them with the rest of us, because she could always get some more.

Failing that we could always play her for them. We were bound to win even though she was probably the cleverest girl in the school. It was said she might even win a scholarship to Christ's Hospital School, although none of us liked the sound of the place. However, girls just couldn't play marbles.

Unfortunately, she made it quite clear she would neither give us any marbles or play us for them. They were hers and would remain so—but we could look at them again if we wanted to. With that she hung up the bag in the cloakroom and flounced off to the upper form, intending to continue being annoyingly clever over something else.

Under normal circumstances anything hung in the cloakroom would have been safe because we were all almost totally honest, having had it beaten into us. The exception was Ian from a lower year, who stole all of our National Savings books and tried to cash them down at the local post office. However, the way Rachel was behaving just wasn't right. Typical of a girl though.

One of the boys, it wasn't me, decided that in the interests of wealth redistribution in the Robin Hood tradition, we should exact a levy of two marbles apiece. It would not hurt and she might not even notice. The bag was almost empty when I took my two and got caught.

The unusual number of eight-year-olds playing marbles in the playground had come to someone's notice and two and two put together—such mathematics being simple for a teacher. I cursed myself for the ten minutes I had spent wrestling with my conscience, but there were many other, otherwise honest, children involved in the great marble heist of forty-seven.

Poor Rachel was deemed to have tantalized us and been boastful and provocative, indulging in more than one of the seven deadly sins. She probably came off worse than the rest of us. She left the school shortly after to go somewhere that specializes in teaching clever, but boastful, people.

Those of us only guilty of the sin of theft, although swearing we intended to give the marbles back, were individually given a good talking to and our parents informed by letter. The headmaster's lenience did not have the desired effect on me. Rather than knuckling down and thanking my lucky stars for my reprieve, I pushed my luck to see how much I could get away with.

Later in the week I was sitting next to Len. Len was fun. He was taller than the rest of us with red hair and an unfortunate habit of being in the wrong place at the wrong time. Being no worse than any other boy it always seemed unjust that he was held up as an example of a wrongdoer. He was a thoroughly nice bloke as well.

A street fire alarm was situated near the gates of the school because with so few people having telephones in those days such devices were essential if a fire was not going to burn for weeks without anyone noticing.

It consisted of a post, about the same height and colour as a letterbox with a sheet of thin glass covering a lever. To sound the alarm, someone would have to break the glass and then pull the lever. Then, as if by magic, the fire brigade would turn up with bells ringing and hoses at the ready.

To the hundreds of small children passing it twice a day there was a temptation to break the glass. In fact, it was broken at least once a month, but no-one ever pulled the lever—knowing what would happen if they did.

The war had been over for two years and many of us were missing the excitement of being bundled into air raid shelters and hearing bombers, guns, and doodlebugs. Even the school had been bombed during the night on one occasion.

I suggested to Len that, lacking anything more interesting to do, and wanting to irritate the establishment, I would break the fire alarm glass on the way home that night. It would make them sit up and take notice. No one would ever know who had been responsible.

The code amongst young boys was strict at that time. It was unthinkable that any of the other boys would snitch on us. Unfortunately, girls were not included in this code.

School was out, and I selected a suitable stone from the roadside. Len and I crept up to the alarm and, making sure there were no adults about, I smashed the glass with the stone and ran like hell.

I looked back and saw Len was not with me. He was still hanging around the alarm. Then, to my horror, he reached in and pulled the lever. I covered the remaining half-mile home in record time, hearing bells faintly ringing in the distance.

I reasoned that the fire brigade had had a pretty slack time since the bombing had stopped, and would probably be glad of the work. I felt smug in my anonymity and relished the anticipation of my enhanced notoriety amongst the other boys. Such pleasant thoughts were interrupted by a knock on the door. A large gentleman in blue stood on the doorstep.

He told my parents what I had done and how his presence at their house was to bring home to their son the gravity of his crime. He left after giving me a stern lecture and assuring my parents that the school would inflict a suitable punishment. There was a long silence after his visit. Father was sitting in the armchair dangerously quiet. Mother had gone into an advanced version of her 'what will people think' mode, and was wondering if, after having a policeman at the door, she would ever dare show her face in the street again. Living on Streatham High Road this would curtail her social life considerably. As for me, I was ignored and considered below contempt.

I had just bought a book called *Fighting the Matabele*, from Jennings second-hand bookshop across the road. That evening I hid in my bedroom reading it. The hero, and the equally heroic Matabele, would never get into trouble for breaking a piece of glass. It was all so unfair.

The unfairness went up several degrees on my return to school the following day. Talk amongst the children was of six fire engines turning up at the school. All lies, there were four at the most, and one of those was just an auxiliary if I were to believe the report of another eyewitness.

However, the general consensus amongst the boys leaned toward the fact that whoever had called them out might cop it. Someone then told me that Ella Ross had seen the culprits and reported them. I was the victim of treachery.

No names were mentioned but people were looking at me strangely. Len then came along to say we were doomed. Ella, who lived in the same street as Len, really had seen and reported us. Furthermore, we were not going to enjoy assembly and prayers this morning. Morning prayers were the traditional time for punishing small boys. Our crime was more serious than any other the masters could remember. Our new fame and notoriety amongst the smaller children seemed little compensation for what was about to befall us.

Being a state school there were certain rules to follow unlike a public school where, it was rumoured, they could beat you to death if the mood should take them. Six strokes on the open hand with a cane, I was assured, was the maximum allowed in a state school — however much the teacher enjoyed doing it.

We couldn't help wondering if they would cane us before or after purging our souls with prayers. We certainly wouldn't fancy putting our hands together after what was about to happen.

The assembly started with the headmaster ranting about the evils of breaking small squares of glass and pulling the levers behind them. And how the people who did this sort of thing would be punished in the afterlife as well as this one. Furthermore, their grandchildren and even the dogs in the street would shudder at the mention of their names. Again, perhaps not his exact words, but something along those lines.

Len looked at me, raised an eyebrow and mumbled, "Pretty grim stuff." He was more used to this sort of thing than I was.

We were then called out for our punishment before the serried rows of children. The infants had the best seats in the house, sitting cross-legged on the floor at the front where they wouldn't miss any of the action.

On the rostrum the teaching staff were sternly looking down on proceedings, like crows on a telegraph wire. It was noted that Miss Sydney, the headmaster's deputy, was standing with the others and not sitting at her piano as she usually was. At least they were not going to do it to music.

We were lucky. I cannot remember who administered the punishment the terror of the moment having erased it from my memory. Mercifully, he had no stomach for the job and didn't put much effort in to it, but the cane was expected to make an audible swish as it came down on our delicate little hands in order to assure the headmaster they were taking the job seriously. He was a very religious man who set great store by the soul-enhancing properties of suffering.

I only received four strokes to Len's six, as it was said his crime was greater as the one who had actually pulled the lever. Apart from that he had bigger hands than me and presented a better target.

We had gritted our teeth and neither of us dared to cry in front of the assembled school, probably one of the cruellest things about it. There was an uncanny silence after the canings. Everyone was holding their breath. I cannot remember if we sang any hymns, we might have already sung them at the start. I just remember the blessed relief as Miss Sydney leaped aboard her piano and started to play Schubert's 'March from Rosamunde', the usual signal for us all to file out of the hall.

The other children gathered around, as was the tradition after canings, eager to see what damage had been done to our hands. We were quite interested ourselves having not dared look for fear there was no damage, and they'd want to do it again. Ken's hands were just a bit red, but I had blue bruises forming in a line across my palm. In the classroom over the following days my writing was somewhat cramped until the bruises had faded.

I was later told that if I could stay out of bad company and try to curb such wickedness, perhaps I had some sort of future ahead of me. But only perhaps.

Years later I was told that Len grew up to be successful—a gentleman and model citizen. I was relieved because I had always felt some guilt over the incident.

Chapter 11: The Dead Pond

About 300 yards from my grandparents' nurseries, in the middle of a field, was a pond. There seemed no logical reason for it to be there. It had a sinister air to it — a nasty sore afflicting an otherwise healthy field.

The water looked dead, but not deep. Three quarters of it was surrounded by sickly trees, and the remaining quarter appeared to be a dug-out extension to the original pond. This was surrounded by unhealthy reeds and protected by a dilapidated wire fence.

My first thought upon seeing any pond was to check its suitability for fishing. Looking at the thick opaque water I doubted any form of life could survive there. It reminded me of the River Graveney back in Streatham but without the green algae. I checked on it each time I came down. It always looked the same — a pool of dark evil-looking liquid hiding some sort of secret. A place of nightmares.

That was, until the hot summer of '49. Everything was different that year. The sun shone incessantly and a heatwave took hold.

The dyke I usually fished, Tenterden Sewer, had almost dried out. There remained a few isolated spots where fish flapped about in the shallows and died in their dozens. Many were dragged out and consumed by other wildlife. Walking along the bank I could see half-eaten roach and the occasional pike on the bank. The rats, stoats and foxes must have been growing really bloated having their own larder from which they could select food at will. It was distressing for me to see so many fish dying. I wondered if my favourite fishing spot, my escape from the horrors of urban life, would ever recover.

It was not long before I slipped and fell in to one of these shallows, while trying to rescue a pike from a few inches of water and relocate it somewhere deeper. I crawled back up the bank covered in mud, leaving the poor pike to its fate.

I appeared at the kitchen door with my legs and trousers caked in swiftly drying mud. Mud that, in that weather, could quickly harden to the consistency of cement. My grandmother lost patience. She told me if I came back one more time in that state, they would send me back to London. Tollgate Cottage was little better equipped than our house in Streatham for continually washing clothes. In fact, water had to be pumped from a well into a storage tank each morning.

Grandfather marvelled at how, in the worst drought in living memory, I had managed to find some mud. Not only found it, but covered myself in it. According to him, only I could have done that.

He was having difficulty finding enough water for the greenhouses and cold frames and had been using a petrol-driven pump to extract water from the small pond excavated for the purpose. That was now nearly empty, so he was working on placing another pump alongside the dyke at the bottom of the hill. The well only supplied the house, and couldn't have supplied the quantities needed to irrigate the crops as well as hose down small boys covered in mud.

Grandmother's threat to send me home made me realize I could easily outstay my welcome.

Usually, when I was staying with them, they rarely saw me between breakfast and supper time. My interest in pond life meant I was always out on the marsh somewhere, either fishing, exploring, or getting covered in mud.

As Tenterden Sewer could not be fished, I rode my bike as far as Appledore to fish the Military Canal. I had to creep past a sign that said, 'No Fishing' and find a secluded spot where no one could see me. I was constantly looking out for bailiffs, and after an uncomfortable couple of hours I had not caught a single fish.

The end of the holiday drew near and I was at a loss for something to do, when I remembered the dead pond. It was bound to be dried out and I could at last solve the mystery of how deep it was, and what, if anything, lay under its murky, black water. With the benefit of hindsight I could always have asked about it. Everybody knew—as I found out later.

The pond looked forlorn without any water, just black decaying leaves from the surrounding trees. It was obvious the main body of it had contained no more than eighteen inches of water at any point. There was a bad smell and I expected to find a rotting sheep carcass nearby, but there was nothing so obvious. Something had definitely poisoned the pond though.

The dug-out extension looked slightly different. The reeds had lost the little greenness they previously had, and had turned brown. The mud was lighter in colour, solid looking, but a maze of cracks where the sun had dried it. It looked much like the parts of the dyke I had been able to walk across.

Looking back, ruefully, I cannot think why I felt compelled to climb over the dilapidated fence and force my way through the reeds. Perhaps I just wanted to walk across the dried mud. There was something strange about the way it differed from the rest of the pond. Or maybe it was the explorer in me wanting to stand on a spot no one had stood on before.

There was no premonition of disaster as I stepped on the cracked mud—just surprise and annoyance as my foot went through the crust and into something soft. This turned to terror as I found myself up to my waist and sinking still further into a morass of something thick, black, and lacking in any obvious charm.

I froze, not daring to move, and not knowing how deep it was. Being a strong swimmer was of little use in these circumstances. The stench alone was making me dizzy. Somehow—pure desperation and fear probably—I twisted round and grabbed the reeds. They still had some substance and this stopped me from sinking further. I then squelched myself into a prone position and laboriously dragged myself out. I lay on the reeds panting, bemoaning my fate, and wondering how it would all end. It was not as if there was any water to wash the worst of it off my legs.

I stopped feeling sorry for myself and trudged back across the field, not expecting to be welcomed by anyone, least of all by my grandmother. It was a horrid-looking evil-smelling creature that appeared at her kitchen door. The worst yet.

It took grandfather some time to hose me down. This was done from a distance with one of the petrol driven pumps providing enough pressure to blast the filth off and chase it down to the nearest ditch. The force of the water came close to knocking me over.

No one wanted to come anywhere near me. Not that I wanted to be near such an awful stinking mess myself, but I had no choice. I was made to strip down to my underpants, much to the amusement of a couple of local people who had wandered round to have a chuckle. Word of my predicament was spreading rapidly.

I heard one of the locals remark, "Reckon he found that old slurry pit in the field over there." A suggestion that was agreed on by all. Sometimes, I thought, there is no substitute for local knowledge. I was going home anyway so I wasn't being sent home in disgrace but I felt I had let my grandparents down.

I had to finish cleansing myself naked in the barn, with buckets of water and a scrubbing brush, before I was finally allowed to get into a warm bath. I was now running out of clothes, and if I wasn't careful, I would have none to travel home in. I vowed that, for the rest of my life if I ever saw anything that looked muddy again, I would give it a wide berth.

I was probably the main topic of conversation that night in the pub across the road, if the laughter I could hear through my bedroom window was anything to go by.

The next holiday found me on my best behaviour. I managed to be helpful and almost saintly, building up loads of goodwill for my next visit. Saintliness, though, did not sit easily on my shoulders and bad luck was always waiting in the wings for me.

Chapter 12: Hospital

The run up to 1950 did not start well for me. I had been feeling unwell and my doctor discovered I had a rare inherited blood condition, called Acholuric Jaundice. Various consultants and surgeons expressed a keen interest in my predicament, and as a result I was packed off to be displayed as 'Exhibit A' in St James' Hospital, Tooting. I spent several months there under observation while, it seemed, every medical student in the world came and poked around my spleen with fingers like icy sausages. 'Why me?' I thought.

In the forties, little information was passed on to a child about his or her illness. It was only the business of the doctor or surgeon in charge. They assumed the child wouldn't understand anyway. It was considered up to the parents to allay any fears the child may have. However, my parents had not been given much to go on, just a few long words they didn't really understand.

Children instinctively know if their parents are being evasive and don't want to tell them something. It was a time of confusion and niggling anxieties for me, but perhaps I also secretly enjoyed the attention.

Further tests showed my younger brother and my uncle on my mother's side also had the condition, but they never suffered any problems from it.

The food in St James's hospital was indescribably awful; lunch often contained cabbage, or something that tasted remarkably like it. The idea started to form in my mind that I was either going to be poisoned or die of malnutrition. The latter option seemed preferable.

I was a fussy eater, always claiming my capacity to enjoy food had been destroyed by mother's wartime helpings of overcooked cabbage. Midday meals had always been an ordeal. The only meal I looked forward to was breakfast. We were allowed to supply and cook our own, having use of a little kitchen by the entrance to the ward. The mobile patients would cook the breakfasts for the bedridden.

As the youngest I was detailed by the other chaps to be waiter. Each morning I dashed around the ward delivering plates and cups of tea to some thirty patients. I was not trusted near the stove, which was very wise of them. My parents kept me supplied with eggs and bacon and the occasional sausage, which were kept in the fridge.

They were strange times. The National Health Service had just been introduced, and some hospital authorities were spending money like drunken sailors. Every week a trolley would come around with bottles of orange squash, lemonade and, unbelievably, syphons of soda water. All free on the health service.

There was only one other boy of my age in the ward and he cottoned on that if we grabbed a couple of free soda-syphons, we could have fun with them. We would try to catch each other asleep in bed and give a quick squirt of fizzy soda in the face. This caused a great deal of noise and chaos down our end of the ward, and bedlinen became soaked. Sister got to hear about it and our supply of soda syphons were cut off at source. But there was still wheelchair racing in the corridor.

I was sent home for a couple of days for Christmas '49. On my return to the hospital things took a turn for the worse. The surgeon decided that my spleen—having provided so much entertainment and joy to medical students from around the world—needed examining more closely. It had to come out and they assured me I didn't really need it anyway. 'They have always wanted to get their hands on it,' I thought, ruefully.

I then found myself in a surgical ward where serious stuff was going on. No soda fights or wheelchair races now. They were in a business that involved knives and things. Everything was so different for a major operation in those days. I woke up sick and in pain, then had a miserable couple of weeks before they would even let me move. I did not feel confident taking my first couple of steps. I was bent double where the long incision in my stomach had healed without me being made to exercise. I crept about like a very old man.

About three weeks after the surgery, they discharged a very different child to the one who had bounced in three months before. I was now a stooping, traumatized mess, and terrified of leaving the hospital. My stomach muscles were going to take ages to recover.

There was worse to come on my return to school. I had never, ever, been bullied— apart, perhaps, from the quacking when I first started at primary school—but that was all to change. A couple of little horrors in a lower year sensed I was damaged and took to tormenting me. It was a very bad part of my life, but they got their come-uppance when I had recovered my strength enough to fight and had grown taller.

The lost schooling did not worry me at first. I stupidly thought I was smart enough to catch up. That was not to be the case. I had been away six months in total at a very important stage in my education. The wider effect of what is now known as PTSD, on a child, was not considered in those days. My ability to learn was impacted for the first year, and the school had no remedial facilities.

I didn't do anything too adventurous for a while. Returning to school at the start of term in September, I found myself relegated to a lower achieving stream.

I was now in a technical group, no longer destined for the higher echelons. However, the good news was that I was going to craft classes. The school had access to really excellent woodwork, technical drawing, and metalwork facilities located a couple of miles away, in Tooting. It meant a tube ride to Tooting Broadway.

At assembly on the first day of term the headmaster lectured us on the evils of amusement arcades. It seems that boys in school uniform had been seen in a Tooting Broadway arcade mixing with the hoi polloi. "This will not be tolerated because those places are sinks of iniquity. Places decent people do not frequent," he said, adding that if any boy from our school was seen there again in school uniform, he would be in Very Serious Trouble. We took that to mean expulsion to one of the secondary modern schools.

My first craft lesson was to be the next afternoon, so I arrived at Tooting Broadway early. It was a vibrant place buzzing with people and activity.

The first thing I saw as I left the underground station was the amusement arcade. There was loud music, and I could see flashing lights coming from machines just inside the door. A group of Teddy boys were playing them. Like many who seek to proclaim their individuality the Teddy boys all looked alike. They had a reputation for violence and disorder, but in truth nothing frightened them more than damaging their expensive clothes. They always looked smart though in their drape jackets, drainpipe trousers and ridiculously thick crepe-soled shoes, with their hair slicked at the sides with Brylcreem, and sporting sideburns and a quiff.

Finding it a fascinating fairyland of light and sound, I entered the portals of our headmaster's idea of Hell's Kitchen. I had to try one of the machines while I was there, thinking no one would know except the Teddy boys.

Slipping off my satchel, I dug deep into my pocket for the coin demanded by the machine. Flashing lights, bells and whistles were all there as I propelled the little steel ball around the colourful obstacle course. It was a fairy-tale place with no trace of the evil the headmaster mentioned. I had to dash away after a second game, realising it was almost time for my technical drawing lesson. I liked technical drawing and unlike other lessons I had not fallen behind.

In the classroom the next morning, I was desperately checking my desk for my satchel, before going into assembly and morning prayers. I couldn't find it and hoped I might have left it at the Tooting classroom. Then Mr Parker called me over. This was always worrying, and the look on his face was not encouraging. "You were in the amusement arcade yesterday, were you not?" he said.

My mind raced. How could he possibly know?

He gave a little smile and told me the Tooting Broadway Arcade owner had visited yesterday afternoon, and dropped my satchel in, saying he found it on his premises. "It was very good of him and he was a nice chap, but I'm afraid the headmaster has your satchel now. Best you get your excuses ready," he advised.

Since my operation I was always leaving things behind. I could hear the great bell of doom clang, as a vision of Mitcham Lane Secondary Modern school leaped into my mind. Would I like it? I looked on the bright side. Most of my mates from the junior school were there.

After assembly, I reluctantly reported to Dick's office. Dick was the boys' nickname for the headmaster, but I never found out why. He looked sorrowful and I waited for the 'This will hurt me more than it hurts you' cliché. It never came. I was given a good dressing down for the amusement arcade incident. He then told me he knew it had been a bad time for me struggling to get back into school life, but he gave no offers of extra help. I promised him I would study hard and stay out of amusement arcades in future.

I later realized there was no real punishment they could have given. What the headmaster had said to the assembled school about the arcade, a perfectly legal and well-run establishment, could have been difficult for him to justify.

As I returned to my form the spectre of Mitcham Lane receded. I was slightly disappointed as I would have liked to have teamed up with my old mates again. And the school had the remedial systems I badly needed.

Chapter 13: School in the Morning

Before TV, we relied on the radio for our Sunday afternoon entertainment. A programme called *Down Your Way* was popular in the nineteen fifties. It was usually on during Sunday teatimes. Franklyn Engleman, a well-known personality of the time, conducted an outside broadcast from somewhere interesting and far away like Leighton Buzzard and other places with names that set a child's imagination rolling.

Was it the smell of strawberries called it to mind? Ah! That's it—that smell. We rarely had real strawberries, but Mother liked to make Sunday teatime stand out from the bread and jam events of weekdays.

She would often make strawberry jelly from mysterious rubbery cubes, and there was cream to go with it, fished from the top of the milk bottle with a thimble on a wire. It was an interesting exercise. Sometimes the thimble would get dislodged from the wire and fall to the bottom of the bottle. Then it was a matter of emptying the bottle to retrieve it, and then waiting for the cream, that had mixed with the milk, to separate and rise to the top again. Just another exciting episode in the boring saga of a post-war rainy Sunday.

There was gold-top milk to thank for the cream. This source was always available after United Dairies delivered a pint of milk with cleaning fluid in the bottom. Mother raised hell about it, and as compensation they would deliver gold-top at the price of standard milk.

Mother would occasionally make a special cake from nuts, biscuits, and melted chocolate if the ration book would allow it. My brother and I loved these cakes, but it was not often all the ingredients were available. Another treat (not rationed) was treacle mixed with bacon fat and spread on slices of bread. A Dutch delicacy.

Mother still had this foreign streak that thirty years in England had not quite bred out of her. Such strange foods were not unusual in our household and mother's exotic background ensured mealtimes could be very enjoyable. Except, of course, when she served up cabbage.

At dinner times during the war mother had often lectured me about our relatives who were starving in occupied Holland. Mother would insist I eat up all my cabbage, because my little cousins would be glad of it. This ensured dinner was a nightmare for me. It also made me imagine little starving children living in windmills, dressed in rags and clattering about in clogs. I could imagine their eager little faces as they held out empty dishes adorned with those blue Delft patterns you find on china windmills and pleading for more in that indecipherable language my grandmother used. Only to be refused and chased away by the stern figure of a Dickensian Beadle—also wearing clogs. Imagination can be a strange and adventurous thing.

Shortly after the war we received a food parcel containing goodies. Goodies that had been unavailable in Britain since before the war and would remain so for some time. There were some things I had never seen before, like chocolate vermicelli. Such luxuries! And from these same relatives I had felt sorry for. I asked Mother how people who had been starving a short time ago could have come by such things. She sounded embarrassed and mumbled something about them having influence and not being short of a bob or two. I thought about the foul cabbage I'd been shamed into eating and felt more than a tinge of resentment.

Back to Sunday teatimes though. A feeling of gloom would descend on me after we had eaten. This gloom was particularly deep in the winter months before I found hobbies, and before we had television.

Gas lighting was miserable. It was not as if you could throw a switch or something. It was necessary to turn on the gas and apply a naked flame, at the same time being careful not to touch the mantle—which would crumble and fall to pieces if you did. You had to wait until the gentle hiss of the gas turned to a just perceptible roar and the mantle glowed brightly. It was advisable to walk around the house after dark with the aid of a candle, which could also be used to light the gas.

With so many naked flames about it would have been a health and safety nightmare. It was wise not to allow children to light the gas lamps as it sometimes resulted in a burned down house, or at the least a broken mantle.

"School in the morning!" Mother would say brightly without regard for the discomfort the thought caused me. At this point I had grown to detest school. I had been unable to play any of the rough games I used to enjoy, and the school had given no help with catching up for the time I had lost. After being near the top of the form for so long, I was bouncing along at the bottom, and each day spent there was an ordeal.

The thought there would be no escape from it until the age of sixteen was always at the back of my mind. I needed to get away from London and the bomb-damaged smoke-blackened buildings. Most of all I needed to get away from that school. It still pains me even to talk about the place.

My illness rumbled on for a couple of years with more time lost at school and constant hospital visits. Had the medicos had got it badly wrong somewhere? There were things I didn't know and never would.

At around fourteen everything seemed to clear up. I was fully fit again and remained so for around forty years.

But to return to the early 1950s. The only mid-week consolations for me were *Dick Barton Special Agent* on the radio, and my love of books. I was an avid reader from an early age. Fortunately, Father used to keep abreast of the current literature and I would read the books after he had. George Orwell's 1984 may have been one of the first adult books I read. There were always a few books in the house, as well as the Beano and Dandy, which I also liked. I haunted the libraries and the second-hand bookshop across the road, for subjects that interested me.

Jennings' bookshop must have been one of the longest-running businesses in Streatham. I remember it before even Ally's Owl Shop—where they sold or swapped almost everything. Except owls! With so much reading and studying the gaps in my education became less obvious. Eventually they were mostly filled, and I learnt to bluff what I didn't know. Things could have been so different though.

A Haydn Wood march introduced *Down your Way*. Whenever I hear it, I am reminded of Sunday teatimes.

Chapter 14: The Breton Onion Seller

I remember one day when I was walking down Streatham High Road in the direction of Norbury with my mother. It must have been 1950 and we were off on the daily shopping trip to Fletcher's grocers. Fletcher's had been our registered grocer since early in the war and we were on friendly terms with them. It was considered wise to be on friendly terms with your grocer in those days.

It must be difficult for many to understand what it was like before homes had refrigerators. We had to shop for something almost every day, but somehow, we managed.

As we trotted along, still in the shadow of bomb-damaged buildings, we were intrigued by a pair of people coming from the direction of the golf links. A perfectly normal-looking woman accompanied by some species of dwarfish creature, so bizarrely dressed it was unlikely to be of this world.

I knew all about aliens, having read extensively about their habits. I was aware that if given half a chance they would dominate the world and destroy the human race just for the hell of it.

I needn't have worried. On getting closer we saw it was a weird and strangely dressed child. Mother made the "harrumph!" noise she usually used to express disapproval, and said, sotto voce, what a dreadful way it was to dress a little boy.

However, as we drew level, we recognized the golden hair and cherubic features of my eight-year-old brother, Adrian. His body was swathed in adult clothes that were far removed from current fashion and hung about him in an unsightly manner. His usually jolly features carried a look of acute embarrassment, as if he wanted the earth to open up and allow him to plunge to oblivion.

I cannot imagine what was going through my mother's mind on realizing the weirdling was her own flesh and blood. Her strong sense of 'What will people think?' must have been fighting with her natural curiosity and motherly instinct. To her credit, she sprang forward and confessed to ownership of the sorry-looking creature.

My brother's keeper turned out to be a kindly soul who had taken pity on the child, after finding it under a bicycle in the River Graveney.

"One can find the strangest things chucked in the river. I once found a dead cat," I piped up, wishing to be involved in a conversation that showed signs of becoming interesting.

She ignored me and told us how she had been alerted by a shout, and a splash, followed by a wail of outrage from the river at the bottom of her garden. Having dredged the little creature from the foul polluted waterway, she and her husband scraped off some of the stinking mud, then took the child indoors to apply medication to its wounds.

Anxious to be shot of the smelly little foundling as soon as possible, she dressed him in a pair of her husband's old shorts and shirt to preserve at least a modicum of decency, before herding him in the direction he claimed to live.

Mother thanked her profusely, while complaining it was the sole aim of her children to worry her to an early grave.

I was sent back with my brother's rescuer to collect his bicycle, while mother took Adrian off to the doctors for some painful injections. I chatted to my brother's saviour about this and that on the way back towards the links. I was trying to create a good impression, but in the process probably being extremely irritating. I gave her an informed opinion on the Berlin Airlift, and the new National Health Service, repeating, of course, things I had heard my parents saying about it during lunch the previous day. We also touched on the proliferation of bicycles in the River Graveney. We wondered about the river's nasty smell, and theorized about the sinister absence of any life forms in its murky waters—other than my little brother of course. I took my leave of the kind lady and pushed home the battered bicycle, leaving her wondering how many other strange children were to be found in the streets and alleyways of south Streatham.

There was no precedent for any member of our family being found under a bicycle in a river so it was with great interest we listened while the little fellow, between drinking copious quantities of lemonade, recounted how he had come to set this new trend.

For no specific reason other than curiosity, Adrian had ridden his bike across the disused golf links that straddled both Streatham and Norbury. We still called it 'The Golf Links' although the hearty fellows who infested it in those ridiculous plus four trousers, fair-Isle jumpers, with shouts of 'Fore' were gone by the mid-nineteen thirties. The beautifully kept greens gradually became a wasteland and four years later fell victim to the government's 'Dig for Victory,' initiative. Like so many pieces of spare land, they became allotments for wartime food production.

To return to Adrian's narrative.

While cycling towards the little bridge that crossed Norbury Brook a few yards before it transmogrified into the River Graveney, his attention had been drawn to an approaching cyclist. "Not the usual sort of Streatham or Norbury cyclist. He was dressed in a beret, striped jersey, and had strings of onions draped over his shoulders, handlebars and panniers," Adrian told us in wonderment.

It was the first Breton onion seller Adrian had seen, and he had been fascinated. Such things were rare in the vicinity of the golf links, even before the war.

He told us how he stopped and sat on his bike with one foot on the low bridge parapet, closely following the progress of this Gallic vendor of alliums. He hoped the strange fellow might do something even funnier than he was already doing.

In his wonder and excitement Adrian lost his footing and tipped over the parapet, plunging some six feet before entering the eighteen inches of rancid, slow-moving water below. As far as we could gather, he wasn't best pleased at finding himself amongst the rubble, old buckets and many other pointy-edged objects that made up the riverbed.

Realizing he was unlikely to drown in water so shallow, he tried to stand up. Covered, as he was, in slime and mud, with nasty things adhering to his clothing, he must have resembled a truncated version of *The Creature from the Black Lagoon*.

The moment he stood up, cruel fate decreed that his bicycle, which had been teetering on the parapet above, should choose that moment to join him. It flattened him back down against the spiky things on the riverbed provoking righteous indignation. It was only then that his cries of rage brought forth a rescuer.

There were no after-effects such as Weil's disease, tetanus or bubonic plague, and the cuts and bruises could hardly be seen after a few weeks. Children were very durable in those days. Over the next weeks he added the experience to his personal store of anecdotes and tales of derring-do, always providing entertainment for awestruck friends and family in the long dark evenings before we had television.

Chapter 15: The Dread Serpent of SW16

It all started when my classmate Ray brought a venomous Italian Swamp Serpent to school. A creature so sinister it even terrified the school bully.

Ray told me, in confidence, it was only a harmless Italian grass snake, but the poor little thing needed some credibility for its own wellbeing.

The snake was for sale, and the price was seven shillings and sixpence. Ray wanted to unload the serpent as soon as possible due his parents giving him an ultimatum, following his mother's screaming fit after making its acquaintance, unexpectedly, while taking some pillowcases from the airing cupboard.

I neither had such a sum about my person, nor were my parents willing to lend it to me. They told me snakes had had a bad press since biblical times and they were unwilling to house a creature carrying such a stigma. And besides, a snake was unlikely to get on with our bald budgie, Choo-Choo. Poor thing was upset enough after its adventure with a glue board set for catching mice.

The problems of an aspiring herpetologist were soon to be solved, however.

It was the Whitsun holiday, and I was to be packed off to stay with my grandparents near Romney Marsh. I spent every holiday there, mainly fishing, or exploring dykes and ponds for interesting wildlife. The place was alive with snakes. Nothing as romantic as an Italian swamp serpent. But the common grass snake grew to an impressive size and could appear menacing to those not versed, as I was, in herpetology.

I had quickly read up on snakes in the *Junior Wildlife Spotters Guide.*

Equipment for gathering serpents presented no problem to a lad like me, having once heard a story where a cobra had been subdued with a forked stick. I cut one from a nearby hedge. Though not really suitable for subduing cobras, it was adequate for my needs. A pair of stout wellingtons and small hessian sack completed the ensemble.

I then felt equipped to face an army of pythons... provided they were small ones.

When I set out next morning whistling a merry snake-hunters song, I had the forked stick over my shoulder with the hessian sack tied to the end, but my oversized wellingtons were making strange squelching sounds. Fearing my quarry may hear them and be warned of my approach, I went back and changed into plimsoles.

Kevin—named thus as I knew no Kevin who would be distressed at having a snake named after him—was sunning himself on the spot where I usually stand to fish. He had probably over indulged in young marsh frogs and was unaware I had become a herpetologist since my last visit. It was clear he hoped to frighten me away by taking that particular spot. Ruining my day's fishing would have amused him.

The poor creature found itself unexpectedly pinned to the ground, held firmly by a forked stick wielded by a child with a look of triumph on his face. Kevin made a dive for safety as the pressure of the stick eased, but found himself in a dark place... The hessian sack was to be his home for the next few days.

After an idyllic life alongside a pretty country stream, unkindly named Tenterden Sewer, Kevin now faced a life of travel, adventure, and uncertainty.

As the Maidstone and District coach rumbled out of Tenterden, I had been fortunate enough to find an unoccupied window seat.

I looked forward to some pond spotting. This was my favourite occupation while travelling on a bus. I would speculate how deep the water might be and what fish it might contain. Dreaming, when I was older and my circumstances improved, of perhaps even fishing it. My enjoyment of this pastime was ruined when a woman of heroic proportions joined the bus when it stopped at the little town of Headcorn.

Seeing a seat only occupied by a small boy, she headed straight for it. She squeezed in alongside me and almost crushed Kevin who was now hanging in the hessian sack between us. I felt Kevin wriggle. The woman must have felt it as well but didn't attach any importance to it. Then came my worst nightmare. The woman wanted to talk to me.

"And where are you going, my little man?" she said in a condescending manner.

For goodness sake! I was twelve years old and had not been called 'little man' since I was five. I was speechless with rage.

"Cat got your tongue?" she added, when my reply was not forthcoming.

I then explained, carefully, and trying to inject a sinister note into my voice, that I was returning to Streatham after spending Whitsun in the country, hunting snakes. I hoped she would not pursue the matter further. "I'm going to be a herpetologist when I grow up," I added, guessing she had no idea what herpetology was. However, she had already registered the word 'snakes,' and all else paled into insignificance.

"Snakes are the spawn of the Devil and I have never known of one to be up to any good," she told me forcefully. "I'm sure that if ever I came across one I, I would drop dead from fright."

People in other seats looked round at this outburst, and I felt Kevin give an embarrassed squirm in his warm cosy nest between our two bodies.

There was no more conversation, and I spent the rest of the time until we disembarked at Maidstone, speculating how they would rescue me from behind her dead body, should she find out what was in the hessian sack.

When I eventually arrived home, in Streatham, there were mixed feelings about Kevin. Mother was sceptical, father was slightly amused, and little brother was disinterested.

An old leaky aquarium we had banished to the greenhouse was designated as a vivarium, and Kevin given its tenancy. I fully intended, after keeping him a week or so, to release him in Mitcham Common swamp. He would like it there. Loads of frogs.

Kevin was some three-foot-long, but less than an inch tall. However, where snakes are concerned long *is* tall. Hardly a day had elapsed before Kevin had slithered over the top of the aquarium, found the gap under the door, and set off to explore the neighbourhood gardens.

It was put about that I had lost my pet snake and it was roaming free across the gardens. My father also let it be known that it was a much-valued pet, perfectly harmless, and any hurt it may suffer would be deeply regretted.

We lived in a row of six cottages with large gardens front and back. Some were overgrown now the wartime Dig for Victory panic was over. Kevin must have lived an interesting and, I like to think, productive and enjoyable life for the rest of the summer.

Hardly a week passed without reports of his activities. Sightings were frequent but he had always gone by the time I arrived with my forked stick and hessian sack. He was unjustly blamed for many atrocities. Some held him responsible for the mangled cat from Hilldown Road. It had obviously been run over by a tram… anyone could see that.

His reign of terror came to an end in early September when there was a knock at our door. A very distressed neighbour from the little cottage three doors down, stood red-faced and weeping on the doorstep. She told us, between sobs, that Kevin was curled up on her garden path and barring access to the toilet. Which, like ours, was at the bottom of the garden.

"I swear I shall get my Alf to take an axe to it when he gets home from work," she threatened.

We allowed her to use our toilet while I gathered up my snake hunting equipment and set out for the scene of the outrage, three doors down. Kevin was, as reported, curled up on her path, enjoying the last rays of the late summer sun. He was convinced he was now the dominant species here in the lower reaches of Streatham and he would never again suffer the indignities of a hessian sack. Wrong, of course.

I took Kevin to school the next day and swapped him with Evans Minor for a book on garden bird recognition. I could now declare myself an ornithologist, having reluctantly given up herpetology because of people's blind prejudice against reptiles.

I was approached by Evans Minor some days later. He complained that Kevin had not been welcomed in the Evans' household. His father, upon hearing what was in the hessian bag, had confiscated it and taken it at arm's length across the street to Tooting Bec Common, where he had released Kevin back into the wild.

"Can I have my book back please?" the little lad asked hopefully.

I then realized there was much wisdom in having chosen a customer smaller than myself. "Push off, Evans," I advised.

Chapter 16: Fall

The following year I was thirteen years old. The recent SW16 serpent outrage, and earlier slurry pit adventure had almost been forgotten. I still had the book from Evans Minor on bird recognition, and my progress towards being a world-renowned ornithologist was well under way. I decided that in spite of my negative experiences with chickens, duck, and a ghastly parrot in the past, I now quite liked birds.

To this end, I purchased a camera from Ally's Owl Shop. As may have been mentioned before, the shop was a well-known Streatham second-hand emporium that swapped, bought, or sold almost everything… with the exception of owls.

No box Brownie for me, the camera he sold me was the goods. It had bellows, and a case that snapped shut. Although, with hindsight, its cheapness should have given me some indication of its quality. It turned out to be pretty useless and let in light where the corners of the bellows had worn away. This gave a sort of dappled effect to the photos.

A good ornithologist laughs at problems posed by primitive equipment, I told myself.

I wanted to wear the camera around my neck wherever I went, hoping to give the effect of a clever young wildlife photographer—one who knew what he was doing and was ready to instantly photograph anything of interest. In reality, it would only be something that hung around for a long time. A slug or snail perhaps. I soon found the camera too heavy carry in that way, and the sore on my neck where the camera strap had chafed took ages to heal after becoming infected.

Whitsun break that year saw me back at Tollgate Nurseries, clicking away at all sorts of things. I discovered a bird had made its nest in a hollow apple tree in the garden and thought I might snap it, if it stayed still for long enough. It didn't.

I then devised a clever plan. I set up the camera on boxes facing the tree and ran a piece of fishing line from the shutter to behind another pile of boxes, where I had to sit hidden. Eventually the bird flashed past, its beak filled with tasty caterpillars. Looking through a crack between the boxes I saw it land on the tree and look suspiciously around before going into the hole, where its hungry chicks were waiting. That was the moment I had been waiting for. I pulled on the fishing line once, then again to make sure the shutter operated. Having pulled too hard the second time, the camera fell to the ground with a crash and the bird flew off. But no matter; I had my first wildlife photo. It would be a couple of weeks before the film was developed and I would know for certain.

The following day I set out for an area called Shirley Moor. A damp expanse of land between Reading Street and Appledore. The camera was left behind because I had no more film. I was a bit short on money, and anyway cycling four miles to Tenterden to buy it didn't appeal.

I had seen a tree on the edge of one of the pastures that possibly contained a pigeon's nest. Never having seen a pigeon's nest up close and in the interest of scientific progress, I needed to examine one. To get to it meant tramping half a mile and crossing fields I knew to be occupied by large, irritable cattle. Carefully skirting along the hedge where one of the fields contained a bull, I made it to the tree without mishap. It was an ancient ivy-covered oak tree of the sort crawling with interesting life forms. It looked easy to climb and I could see the untidy pile of twigs that made up the nest. It was close to the top. However, reaching it should be no problem for an almost fit thirteen-year-old.

It was an easy climb, until I reached the point where the nest was just above my head. I just needed to be a couple of feet higher, but there was no handy branch. 'These birds know what they are doing when the build their nests,' I told myself. A thick branch of ivy was just in the right place, and, although warning bells were ringing in my head, I ignored them. I had forgotten just how high up I was. I grabbed the ivy and tried to pull myself up. There was a tearing sound as the ivy came away from the trunk. I looked desperately for something solid to grab… but there was nothing.

The next solid thing I was to encounter was a branch halfway to the ground. I hit it with a sickening thud that spun me around until I was watching the sky. In this position I continued rapidly towards the ground, mercifully unable to see the speed of its approach.

I have no idea how long I was unconscious. All I knew was my head and back hurt when I came round and I was possibly not dead. I tried calling for help, but it was pointless and hurt me to do it. I was in a remote spot and no one would have been within half a mile, or further, of me. 'Sod ornithology,' I thought.

As my numbness and terror subsided and I could breathe again, I was relieved to find I could move my back. More of the numbness wore off and I found my legs were okay as well. 'I might have got away with it,' I thought. I tried to get myself to a sitting position and discovered I had not escaped unharmed. My arm was badly broken and the hand and wrist joint were dangling obscenely from a messy-looking fracture.

I eventually managed to stand up and start the painful journey home. I walked straight past the fearsome bull I had been so cautious of on the way there. The creature just glanced at me disapprovingly. No leaping over the gates this time. I had to carefully open them and close them behind me. Not easy when trying to support a dangling arm.

My grandmother was to suffer another nasty shock at the kitchen door as a forlorn, and really second-hand-looking child appeared. She should have been getting used to it by now.

Grandfather drove me to Taylor-Jones, their family doctor in Tenterden, where I was given painkillers. Then on to Ashford hospital where I was put to sleep and my arm hurriedly set. A couple of days later they had to break it again to do the job properly.

I was not enjoying my summer break and was fast losing interest in ornithology. A nurse had, unkindly—despite my denial—accused me of birds-nesting and expressed disapproval. I was sure they were going to torture me if they got the chance.

Sympathy for my predicament was in short supply. The plaster remained in place for six weeks after I returned to London.

On returning to school I was not able to master the art of writing with my left hand, so was assigned the job of 'Form Storyteller' having to make up a suitable yarn during each English lesson. It turned out to be useful training in later life.

If you are wondering about the wildlife photo I took earlier, it actually came out. Amongst the dappling from the light leakage you could just see the tail of a bird disappearing into a hollow tree. I still have the photo somewhere. As for the camera… although useless it was attractive enough for someone to steal some years later.

My studies of the natural world had not proved successful, and another pastime now had to be found.

Chapter 17: Room 101

All the portents of doom were present as I dawdled reluctantly from the cheerful bustle of Tooting Broadway, and down Garret Lane to meet my Nemesis. I was not sure of the time, having lost my watch, but I knew I was early. It was a depressing road and I could think of nothing at my destination that was going to give me any joy. I wanted to be back in the pleasant surroundings of the tube station. I liked tube stations. I especially liked the Art Deco lines of the buildings and the plain readability of the signs and maps set into the walls. Balham tube station, where I had travelled from, was the only thing worth looking at in the entire suburb.

Attached to a crumbling static water tank, that occupied a gap where a house had once stood, there was a blitz-scarred building bearing the dread words: *Wandsworth Schools Clinic*. 'Childe Roland to the dark tower came.' The words and artist's images of the tower in Browning's *Childe Roland* sprang to mind. I don't know why. The clinic was nothing like the image, but the words had stuck in my mind from a recent school lesson and were suitably sinister.

The door was dark brown with a cracked pane of glass. 'Some poor devil trying to escape,' I thought gloomily. The waiting room walls were green with wooden benches against them, the whole place having an all-pervading smell of disinfectant and fear. The door closed behind me with an unexpected bang, alerting a grim-looking harridan who was crouched over a desk. She was writing what I imagined to be death warrants.

"Name?" she said curtly, continuing to write without looking up. I nervously gave my name. The harridan pointed to the uncomfortable-looking benches along the opposite wall. I took this to mean I could sit down. The lady was certainly economical with words. I suspected she just didn't like her job and hated children. I stared at her from my hard and unyielding seat, trying to make my stare seem accusatory because I knew from experience that adults didn't like this.

'Perhaps she only knows only one word of English,' I thought, in mitigation.

I hadn't believed my classmate Bill's stories about the London County Council employing Nazi war criminals at the school clinic. Now I was beginning to wonder. He did live just down the road and his claim to have seen bodies being smuggled from the back door could not be entirely discounted. Although his stories of hearing screams and sobs above the sound of marching jackboots may have been taking things too far.

I tried to reason with myself. Bill had a vivid imagination and had been known to lie. In fact, he almost always lied. Things like that just didn't happen in England now the war was over. Did they? This was Tooting though, and the people around here lived by their own rules.

My fears regarding my possible fate were now deeply rooted in my psyche, and would certainly cloud whatever events followed. I cursed my stupidity at complaining about toothache while at school. I had thought it a good wheeze for dodging double maths that afternoon. I actually had got a slight toothache but had put up with it for over a week, saving it until it could be usefully employed. I had expected them to send me home to the family dentist.

There were noises from the treatment room, followed a raised adult voice. Gentle sobbing could just be heard behind the buzz of the drill. When the door opened a boy of about ten came into the waiting room, still snivelling, with tears streaming down his face. "You can stop that noise. You're not a baby!" snarled something primeval from the treatment room.

Still not looking up or speaking, the desk harridan stopped scribbling and held out the child's new appointment card.

Like the crack of doom my name was called, and in a daze of trepidation I walked into the brightly lit, white and green surgery. The dentist's appearance confirmed my worst fears. He was small and sinister, with little round Heinrich Himmler spectacles. Across the room a dangerous-looking nurse was happily arranging instruments of torture on a tray, whilst humming something Wagnerian. I fervently hoped the last victim had sated their appetite for sadism.

I bore the horrid vibration of the drill stoically, not daring to make a sound. It was obvious, looking around me, that the dental equipment was not as modern as that used by our family dentist. The drill ground on slowly. 'Probably second-hand and blunt,' I thought, and wondered how many unpleasant mouths it had been in before. A filling was put in one of my cuspids after a suitable pit had been laboriously ground out by the drill.

I formed the impression that I was just another small inconvenience to be processed and sent on its way. As I left the chair the nurse muttered the words, "Good boy." This would have been comforting had it been directed at *me,* rather than directed to the wall like a well-practised mantra. Apart from "Open vide!" Himmler had not said a word during the treatment and I had the uncharitable thought that he was probably dreaming about happier days in the Third Reich.

Glancing at the stony face of the desk harridan on the way out. I wanted to shout, '*Heil Hitler*,' but, unexpectedly, she smiled at me. Her face lit up and laughter lines appeared at the corners of her eyes, transforming her into an entirely different person. She even put the pen down. "Hope you have no more trouble with the tooth my dear. Take care," she said. I felt like a complete rotter for my previous train of thought.

Children can be very impressionable, and I believe some school clinics had a reputation for insensitivity. The fact remained—I would have crawled into a corner and died rather than complain of any ailment at school again.

Chapter 18: A Fourpenny Bus Ride

My swimming trunks were rolled up in a white towel and I had a whole shilling to spend. After bus fare to the swimming baths and my entrance fee, I knew there would be enough for two slices of bread and dripping at bus station café… if I walked home.

Mother would go mad if she knew I was buying bread and dripping. "People will think I don't feed you proper food," she would say. I had yet to find out who these people were who watched her behaviour so closely.

I was conscious of the sharp smell of chlorine invading my nose and mouth as I entered Streatham baths with my friend Bill. Even when my ears popped on the way home, I would be able to smell and taste it.

Then there was the smell of the changing rooms, a mixture of chlorine, sweaty feet, and bodies. The men's communal changing rooms at Streatham baths were unpleasant for many reasons, and we hated them. Strange men used to sit there, never going into the pool or getting wet. They just sat, wearing their bathing trunks, smoking, and, of course, watching us while we changed. Their eyes seemed to be everywhere. There was always at least one there. I remember one fellow being challenged by a member of the staff. He simply relaxed along the bench and said he had just come down there for a smoke. These people were never thrown out, but it was rumoured one of them got a good thumping from one of the boys' father. Even at that age we had a sort of jungle telegraph—suspect men like that were noted by us and avoided.

If it had been warmer, we would have gone to Tooting Bec outdoor pool. They have individual changing cubicles there and a café. It was a bit late in the year for open air swimming though, and in a few weeks even Streatham Pool would be emptied out, boarded over, and used for dances and functions. Swimming would then be over for the winter.

It even felt cold for an indoor pool that day. They were probably economizing on the heating and I wished they would economize on the chlorine instead. We always came out of the pool with red eyes.

I could not bring myself to just plunge into the water that day. I gently lowered myself in from the steps, feeling the creeping cold as the water reached my belly, then my chest. I plunged my head under to get it over with before swimming briskly to the far side and climbing out. There is only so much you can do at a swimming pool, unless you are training for something, or learning to swim. Us lads would follow a sort of ritual to acclimatize ourselves. Next on the list was to dive in and swim the 10m width of the pool underwater. The chlorine content of the water made it best to keep your eyes closed as long as possible and only open them in time to avoid hitting the other side. It always hurt more under water.

I had been able to swim strongly since the age of eight. A family friend had regularly taken me to the baths for lessons and the water held no terrors for me. I felt at home in it.

Next thing on our schedule of activities was diving. I seem to remember them having a three-metre board and only about two meters of water below it. This made it safer to jump off than to dive. It was surprising how few people used the high boards. One of the dangers was that people swam underneath them. There were lifeguards on duty to prevent this, but they were always chatting up and showing off to girls, instead of looking out for the safety of swimmers. I had had a couple of close shaves when I had tried to run along and dive from the top diving board. A dangerous thing to do because you lose sight of anything below it. Fortunately, few people were stupid enough to do this.

Looking down at the pool from the end of the top board it looked the size of a handkerchief. The shouts of the bathers amplified by water and empty space tended to be hard on ears already irritated by chlorine. I had dived off this board a hundred times but still had a mild panic attack when I stood on the end. I somehow felt that people were looking at me and if I chickened out there would be shouts of derision from everyone.

I followed the accepted procedure. I tested the bounce while standing on the edge, then two steps backward, leap forward land squarely on the end and launch myself into space. Then fold, touch toes and straighten just in time to enter the water cleanly. I entered it too cleanly, because I was showing off and possibly thought I was diving at Thornton Heath pool, where there was 15 feet of water. I was moving too fast and the water was too shallow for this sort of dive. I spread my arms to slow down but it was too late. My face struck the bottom.

I saw stars. There were black lines, white tiles, and red swirling blood. My face was numb from the blow. My lungs hurt. 'Mustn't open my mouth,' my instincts told me. 'Must get to the surface... everything is blurred... must get to surface and climb out.' Then, somehow, I was at the at steps and Bill was helping me out. The lifeguards had not noticed because they were concentrating on chatting up some girls.

They were still talking to the girls as I staggered past them feeling sick, dizzy, with blood pouring from a broken nose. Only Bill helped me to the changing rooms. There were no staff anywhere—all probably talking to girls.

One of the strange men in the changing room came to help. 'I must not talk to him... *Never* talk to strange men.' Mum, Dad, and my teachers had all told me, "Never, ever, speak to, or go with, anyone you don't know."

I dressed hurriedly, not bothering to dry myself. My clothes stuck to me as I rushed out of the building to the bus stop. I must have looked like a victim of a car crash or someone who had had a disagreement with a mad axeman. A couple of people glanced at me and then quickened their stride, not wishing to get involved.

Bill was still with me, worried by the blood. My towel and shirt were red. I went straight home on the bus after assuring the conductor I was not about to bleed any more, or die and cause him reams of paperwork.

To his credit, he declined to take a fare and I almost toyed with the idea of going back for my bread and dripping at the café. Instead. I decided to forgo it and return straight home to nurse my broken nose,

The following day at school I had two black eyes and looked remarkably panda-ish. The teachers probably assumed I had been fighting and didn't ask me about it. In those days they did not seem so concerned about children's welfare. Whether there was less cruelty or less awareness of it is hard to say.

Chapter 19: Model Aircraft

It was 1951. I was thirteen years old and desperate to own a miniature diesel engine. I watched them every weekend on Mitcham Common and I was fascinated. They were easily the noisiest toy known to mankind, and endearingly smelly.

Model aircraft were fast becoming my main interest. They were to be my introduction to engineering and, eventually, the fascinating world of motorised transport... until pubs, then girls, inevitably took over in later years. But, having been sent to a boys-only school and having no sisters or young female relatives, girls still seemed like an alien species to me in my early teens and I, reluctantly, stayed out of their way.

I turfed all evidence of keeping smelly little animals out of my bedroom and the lean-to greenhouse. The chickens had long gone, as you could buy as many eggs as you wanted. The only livestock remaining was a stubborn mouse behind the front room skirting board. And its luck would run out soon enough when mother saw it. Only the fishing tackle remained. There was no way I was going to give up fishing.

Sheets and blocks of balsa wood, and tubes of smelly and highly flammable glue were bought from the modelers shop opposite the ice-rink, and books and magazines on the subject of model-making now littered the house.

I started by building little hand-sized models of WW1 biplanes. They could not fly, but to my mind made nice ornaments. After my trips to Mitcham Common to see the efforts of others, I then graduated to fragile, rubber-powered, tissue covered aircraft that were supposed to fly. These were fiddly and time consuming to make considering they smashed with the first strong breeze to catch them. Then I moved on to scale models with noisy little diesel engines.

I ultimately built a tiny radio control transmitter and receiver that actually worked. But I never fitted it to an aircraft because by then other interests were taking over. The fact that I had managed to do it impressed a few people though.

It was said that the larger powered model aircraft could actually kill someone, if encountered unexpectedly at high speed. There was an irresistible aura of fun and danger about them.

One of the cheapest model engines available was called the 'Bee,' and was made by a company called ED. It cost two pounds and fourteen shillings. This was the wrong time of year for a Christmas or birthday present, but I had to have one. Ally's Owl shop again came to my rescue. I spotted, in the corner of the window, an ED Competition Special. It was a slightly dated motor, but simple and reliable. He let me have it for £1.

I was over the moon and couldn't wait to alienate the neighbours by starting it up in the back garden. However, first I needed fuel. Although a tin of ready-made fuel was available from the model shop, real enthusiasts always proudly made their own for a fraction of the cost.

One just needed the ingredients. The first was paraffin, which was dirt cheap, and everyone had some in their sheds. The second was castor oil, which could be bought from the chemist. The third was ether. Unbelievably, it could also be bought from the chemist, even by a thirteen-year-old boy. They even, on one occasion, sold me amyl nitrite for an added boost to the fuel!

The little lean-to greenhouse in the back garden became a centre for scientific progress, with chemicals being mixed in jars and loud bangs as the engine backfired again, and failed to start.

I was finding the whole thing quite confusing for a while. Then I had the bright idea of leaving the greenhouse door open so my brain received a lower dose of ether. It started working again. One small adjustment. Then I flicked the propeller and the engine started with a mighty howl—bringing all the neighbours into their back gardens thinking the doodle bugs had returned.

Father and Mother were not pleased. Mother once more went into her 'What will people think?' mode. She made me promise to only start the thing on the common, or the old golf links. Much of her anger passed over my head owing to the ether still freezing my brain, coupled with the pain from my index finger which had been severely rapped by the propeller every time the engine had backfired. It was starting to look like an undercooked chipolata.

I had learned a lot from my experiments in the greenhouse and started to address the problem of a suitable aircraft kit for the engine. Money was a problem as usual. Buying the engine and fuel had wiped out what was left of my morning paper round money. The answer was to take on an evening paper round as well, to swell my weekly income and, with luck, two lots of Christmas tips could be collected. I would be able to afford a model kit and a flash new up-to-date motor come the new year.

I had joined a club in Mitcham called the Park Model Aircraft League, who met in a local school. The club was mostly adults, but there were a few of us teenagers.

It was the first real club I had belonged to, apart from a very short membership of the Wolf Cubs where I had been expelled for fighting, and the Boys Brigade, where they actually expected me to pray. I left after the Christmas party, mainly because I had never been given a trombone to play in the band.

Many friendships were formed at the Model Aircraft Club and there was always something interesting going on. Round the pole flying was one of the best. There was not enough space in the hall to use flying diesel engine planes as we did on the common. However, RTP was a fascinating substitute. The aircraft we used were crude, made out of cigar tubes with wings glued to the side. Propulsion was by the dreadful 'Jetex' motor. This consisted of a machined aluminium barrel loaded with a pellet of solid rocket fuel. It was sealed by powerful springs, securing an end cap with a small vent for it to jet from. A fuse of explosive covered wire passed through the vent to ignite the rocket fuel. One only had to strike a match to start an interesting, smelly, and possibly dangerous chain of events.

We sometimes had half a dozen of these competing in the hall, and the smoke and smell could be quite alarming. It hung in the air all evening like a smelly fog and was still there when we left at nine o'clock. I often wondered if it could have been why we lost the use of the school hall.

On Sundays, we flew our models on Mitcham Common, an altogether more suitable venue. Control line flying was popular at the time, with radio control still in its infancy. Free-flight, where the model was set free to fly where it liked, was going out of fashion. A change in wind direction could sweep your prized aircraft out over the suburban sprawl of Mitcham, where it often landed in one of the many surrounding graveyards… if you were lucky. At dusk on a winter's afternoon, when walking past one of the graveyards it was not uncommon to be scared witless by someone appearing unexpectedly from behind a tombstone. On occasions he might be holding a badly damaged model aircraft.

On my first trip to Mitcham Common I had met Brian, a very accomplished aeromodeller and owner of more than one engine. Such wealth. We were to become lifelong friends and share many amusing adventures.

Chapter 20: The Red Panther

Sixteen at last. I left school and became an apprentice in Brixton. Not far away, in Stockwell Road, was the 'Red Valley'—a row of buildings on each side of the road, all painted red. It was also known as Pride and Clarke Ltd., Motorcycle Dealers. Another place of wonder and magic for a teenager, almost on a par with Ally's Owl Shop.

It is hard to describe to anyone but a fellow enthusiast, the beauty and clever mechanical innovation of a thirties or forties motorcycle. Many of the engines are pure sculpted art. Pride and Clarke had hundreds of them for sale. From a £25 ex WD Royal Enfield to the latest new superbike.

I had to have a motorbike. One I could ride to work, or even use to visit my grandparents in darkest Kent. That would be quite an adventure. The problem was that as an apprentice I was only earning fifty-four shillings a week. I was actually poorer than when I had done two paper rounds while at school.

From what I now earned I had to pay my parents for my keep, my bus fares to work and buy the odd (illegal) pint in the local. But if I thought the cost of buying a motorcycle presented a problem, I was yet to find out about the cost of insurance and road fund licence.

Before the war, Pride and Clarke had marketed a reliable motorcycle for £27.10s. I spotted an envelope in a shop window offering one of them for sale. £10 was asked. The bike was seventeen years old.

However, at that time you could subtract at least six years for being laid up during the war, and there were always petrol shortages to keep mileage in check.

The vendor lived in a one-roomed ground floor flat with his wife and baby, in a Brixton backstreet. There was an air of squalor and desperation you could not fail to notice. He took me to the hedge at the front of the house where the bike was half buried in the foliage. My friend and I helped him pull it out. The hedge was reluctant to let go, as if it and the bike had formed a bond. After fitting the battery and priming the carburettor it started immediately.

Having been left out there for some time it was looking a bit rough, but I couldn't bear to haggle with him as he obviously needed the money desperately. He couldn't deliver the bike, having lost his license. I pointed out it would be hard work for me and my friend to push it over Brixton Hill to Streatham. I was not insured and didn't even have a provisional license. Not to mention that I had never ridden a motorbike in my life.

"Not a problem," he said. "Just start it when you get to the hill, put it in first gear, let out the clutch and run alongside it. When you have to go down Streatham Hill, just sit on the saddle and freewheel with the engine switched off. In neither case will you be riding a powered machine." Luckily, the legality of this was not put to the test. The police must have been having a lunchbreak or looking the other way.

I arrived safely home, having used the method he suggested, with my friend running along behind me. At times I actually rode the bike under power when temptation overcame caution. I now considered myself to know all about riding a motorbike and needed no further lessons. With some help from my parents I managed to scrape together the money for insurance, tax, and a licence. I was now the proud owner of a road-legal 1937, 250cc Red Panther.

There was just one more expense. A helmet. It was not a legal requirement then, but there was no way mother was going to let me ride the bike without one. Luckily, they bought me one as an early birthday present.

There were a few mishaps and scrapes with the bike over the following weeks. The worst was caused by a badly adjusted hand change mechanism, and my own stupidity.

It was difficult to get into first gear because the mechanism was out of adjustment, so I tended to leave first gear engaged whenever possible. I was stationary at a junction, and about to join the Streatham Vale Road from alongside Streatham Common Station, when I happened to look down at the engine. I spotted the knurled nut was coming unscrewed where it held the high-voltage lead to the sparking plug. I feared that if it came off it would be lost.

Not wishing to come out of first gear I held the clutch in with one hand, and reached down to tighten the screw with the other… and me an electrical engineering apprentice?

It was like being kicked by a horse, as several thousand volts went through me. My hands jumped from the handlebars, releasing the clutch and somehow twisting the throttle at the same time. The bike went one way and I went the other. I landed in the gutter and the bike ended up in the middle of the road. Fortunately, there was little damage apart from to my pride. I fervently hoped no one I knew had seen the performance.

After getting a handbook from the library, I scrounged some tools and did maintenance on the machine, managing to make it reliable enough to get to and from work.

I also started to make regular fishing trips to Hampton Court, East Molesey and Shepperton. I fell off it a couple more times because of skidding on bald tyres.

The day arrived, when I was to ride it to my grandparents in Kent. Mother packed me a flask and sandwiches and I sorted out and packed a tool kit, in case of mechanical problems. I considered myself prepared for anything when I set off at six o'clock that morning, making it to West Wickham in about twenty minutes. There I found I had forgotten to fill the tank. It was Sunday, and I had to wait outside a garage until it opened at nine am. Oh dear.

The journey was only fifty-five miles in total and I should have been safely at my grandparents by eight that morning. It was mid-morning by the time I arrived, having had an uneventful journey apart from waiting for the garage to open. Grandmother had already started to panic when I turned up at that kitchen door unharmed—and not covered in mud for a change.

During the winter I bought a newer machine. A 1947 AJS 16m. It looked smart, had telescopic forks and was more powerful. The faithful Panther had to go, so was advertised in the local newsagent's window. At eight pounds, I was losing a couple of quid but what the hell, I had had a year of fun from it. A studious-looking lad with horn-rimmed spectacles answered the advert. He showed an interest and actually waved £7.10s in front of me. Deal done.

"Don't know how I'm going to push it to the top of Valley Road," he lamented. "I've never ridden a motorcycle."

"Easy," I told him. "Just start the motor, select first gear, and run alongside holding the handlebars…" I never saw him, or the bike, again.

Chapter 21: Austin Ten

My friend Brian bought himself a car. It must have been sometime in 1955 if I remember correctly. It was a sturdy little beast but my description of it as a car was not exactly accurate. It was a 1932 Austin 10/4 Van.

It had cast iron disk wheels which gave it an even more solid appearance. Windows had been cut into the sides to give the impression of a shooting brake, also giving inmates a little daylight to allow them a quick glimpse of anything the car was likely to hit.

As I recall, our first adventure with it was a trip to a Model Aircraft Show at Woburn Abbey in Bedfordshire. It was an ambitious trip that included going through the centre of London. A trip that, even if made in a much younger and well-maintained car, many in those days would consider an epic. There were still a few question marks about the Austin though. It *was* twenty-three years old but came with someone's assurance it was a good runner. So that was okay then.

Brian, and Dusty—another friend from the model aircraft club—plus myself and several model aircraft were packed inside the car, and we burbled away from Brian's home in Mitcham and into the London traffic. We were in high spirits. Dusty was sitting alongside Brian clutching a sinister-looking blue chemist's bottle. I was to find out what it was later. Otherwise, the sun was shining and all was right with the world.

All was going well, until we encountered a steep hill in north London, and the Austin's clutch started to slip alarmingly. We crept towards the top of the hill with the engine screaming and slowing all the time. Those driving behind started to sound their horns. I was to find out, years later, when I owned an Austin Ten myself, that the clutch was one of the only weaknesses on an otherwise 'bulletproof' vehicle.

Brian had experienced the problem before and had made provision for it. The inspection cover above the clutch had been left open and Dusty proceeded to pour the contents of the blue bottle on to the spinning clutch and flywheel. The inside of the car filled with evil smelling smoke and fumes, followed by a great deal of coughing and a dash to open the windows. The good news was the clutch stopped slipping and we sped on up the hill with our throats burning and eyes watering. "Carbon Tetrachloride... Never fails." Brian shouted cheerfully between coughs. We made it to Woburn Abbey with no further problem. It was not until some years later that we learnt we had survived a poison gas attack of our own making.

It was a great model aircraft show in a fantastic location. We just had time to explore some of the grounds before the day's events.

Brian had entered the control line team races and I assisted as motor starter. This involved me squirting fuel into the aircraft's tank from a supply contained in an old car horn rubber bulb with a spout attached. I then had to flick a sharp wooden propeller, attached to the engine, until it fired and started with a howl. The plane was then released to dash around with all the others... until it ran out of fuel, then we would repeat the process. It was great fun but could be hard on the index finger when the engine backfired.

I had, myself, brought a control line scale model of a HE113 fighter I had made a year or so earlier. Possibly the last model I made. I had laboriously scaled up the plans from a silhouette in an aircraft recognition book, spending many weeks and no small amount of money building it. Strangely enough, I later discovered the real aircraft never actually existed. I'd made a model of a myth.

Sadly, I had made a mistake in constructing the control line fulcrum plate and the plane piled into the tarmac after completing one circuit. It was going to be a long job rebuilding it, but that was the part I used to enjoy. I don't believe I bothered in this case as I had other things to do, and model aircraft were, for me, becoming a thing of the past by this time.

The journey home was fun. We stopped at a pub halfway home for a pint, a sandwich, and a game of darts. We experienced Keg Bitter (stored in a pressurised aluminium keg) for the first time. We thought we liked it. The ale was claimed to be a uniformly good-tasting drink wherever you bought it and even an idiot pub manager could keep it in good condition. Ales straight from a wooden barrel could be variable, depending on the skill of the cellarman.

It was not long before we began to detest the taste of keg ale and yearn for the real stuff from the wooden barrel. Whatever its failings.

There was another adventure yet to come in that sturdy old car—a trip to Hastings, in darkest

Sussex. We had no concept of fear in those days. I am not sure if we actually intended to go to Hastings, but the trip sort of developed as we found ourselves further and further from home. I discovered motoring to be a less exhausting and dryer way of visiting a place and looked forward to getting a car myself.

We parked up and went to explore the town. As lads will do, we found our way up the nearby cliffs, and I, in the mistaken belief that it was safe—reinforced by the effect of couple of pints I had drunk—tried to get down to a lower shelf of chalk. I slipped down until I found myself between a sheer drop to the beach, and an unstable bank of shale above me. It was normally something I would have scrambled up with no trouble, but the knowledge that a slip would be fatal put me off.

I remained rooted to the spot for a long time while Dusty heroically ran the mile back down the cliffs to the car and brought back the tow rope.

My short life flashed before me several times as I clung precariously to that cliff edge, but holding on to the rope to stop me slipping as I scrambled back up made me feel something of a fraud. It was so easy.

We stopped for a drink on the way home at a pub called The Old Vauxhall, on the outskirts of Tonbridge. When we returned to the car and started it, there was no drive. Just a racing engine and a whirring sound.

We found a woodruff key had sheared in a rear hub. An easy and cheap problem to rectify. Normally. Not on a Sunday evening in the wilds of rural Kent though. We went back into the pub and discussed the problem over another pint. We must have still been over thirty miles from home and catching a bus didn't seem an option.

Brian phoned a workmate who owned an MG TC, and the splendid chap recklessly agreed to come down and tow us back to Mitcham.

The MG sports car was never designed to tow something double the weight of itself, let alone something with people in it, but it managed heroically. The Austin was towed back to Mitcham. It took ages.

It was very late that night when I collected my bike and cycled home to Streatham. Another good day out, with a spot of excitement thrown in. There was little doubt that cars could be fun, but it would be a couple of years before I had my own.

Chapter 22: Brighton or Bust in Indigo Shorts

For people living in London, a trip to Brighton always held a certain magic. People went there in groups, in veteran cars from the earliest part of the twentieth century. This excursion celebrated the redundancy of all the fellows who had previously had to walk ahead of them carrying a flag. It is a fact that only the British could put a vehicle on the road capable of over 30mph, then insist a man walks ahead of it.

But all of that foolishness ended in November 1896, when they celebrated *The Locomotives on Highways Act.* This act allowed the Toad of Toad Hall types to cut loose and have, 'The Great Emancipation Run' from London to Brighton. This run was revived in 1927 and has run most years since. It is the largest gathering of pre-1905 cars known to take place anywhere in the world. In London they christened it, 'The Old Crocks Race'. But in no way was it supposed to be a race, and the meticulously restored vehicles were anything but crocks.

Every year, on the first Sunday in November, my brother and I would get up early to see the veteran cars going past our house. We could watch in comfort from the window of our parents' bedroom, shouting with excitement as strange, then even stranger vehicles appeared. It would entertain us for an entire Sunday morning. They would often break down outside our house. We would then put on warm clothes and dash out to have a closer look at them, but soon learnt to keep our distance from the drivers. The fellows were often quite irritated at breaking down a couple of miles from the start and likely to shout at any youngster getting in the way. There was something elegant about Edwardian cars, they truly caught the transition from horse to engine. I vowed that one day I would own something similar.

I never had the chance to go to Brighton by veteran car, or even have a dirty weekend there, which was another activity beloved by Londoners. However, in 1955 I took part in an epic cycle ride to Brighton with a couple of mates. It was a strange thing to do as I had a perfectly serviceable motorcycle parked in the garden. None of my friends, however, showed any interest in owning motorised transport and I could hardly cheat by using it.

"Let's do this properly chaps and wear shorts. All serious cyclists do, and we may be able tag on to a club run somewhere," suggested Jack, whose idea the run was.

Jack was a friend from my primary school days and our friendship had been renewed through model aircraft, and fishing. We also had common interests in beer and girls. Frank— who was a colleague of Jack's at a London publishing house—and I would have rather been seen dead in a ditch than wear shorts. But we somehow failed to mention that to Jack.

My family were living temporarily in a prefab in Grasmere Road, near Streatham Common, while new flats were being built where our old house had been. Being close to the High Road, which also happened to be the A23 to Brighton, we started from there.

Jack turned up, as promised, wearing a new pair of blue cycling shorts. All I could think of saying was, "Nice shade of blue."

"Indigo, actually," he told us, giving us the sneaking suspicion that the whole trip was just a ploy to show off these cycling shorts. However, before the day was over, he was to bitterly regret wearing them, and not only because of our humorous banter concerning his pale naked legs.

I remember passing through Norbury, about a mile down the road, and asking Jack how much further it was. "Still over fifty miles to go," he shouted cheerfully. He was putting great reliance on the athletic advantages of wearing indigo shorts.

Neither Frank nor I had planned on going much beyond Purley. Perhaps the Airport even. We stopped and had a hearty and leisurely breakfast after passing it. As we found ourselves further away from Streatham, where we had started, things were looking serious. Jack was showing no sign of flagging, or even starting to lose enthusiasm. We were surprised when we found ourselves at Coulsdon, where we stopped for another cup of tea.

On reaching East Grinstead for lunch there was dissent in the ranks as Frank and I suggested it was time to start for home. We had cycled a long way and consequently it was a long way back home to Streatham.

"We're over halfway now and it's downhill all the way to Brighton. We may as well finish the trip," said Jack optimistically, egging us on. He added, "We can take it easy on the way home. Perhaps have a meal and a few drinks on the way."

The young have no concept of time and planning. At least *we* didn't. We grudgingly agreed to go on a little further, perhaps having yet another cup of tea at the next café.

'Downhill all the way to Brighton.' Those words were to haunt us as we struggled with hill after hill… all going upwards it seemed. We stopped at the top of one of them while I shared out the remains of my secret stock of glucose tablets. It was too late to turn back now. We had no lights and it would be dark long before we got home. It would even be dark before we reached Brighton if we didn't hurry. We had approached the trip in a casual and disorganised fashion and were paying for it. We had stopped for too many cups of tea, and as a result had to stop every few miles for a pee as well.

There was talk of sleeping under the pier and cycling back to London in the morning. Jack was not keen, complaining his indigo shorts would give him little comfort in the small hours on a draughty beach.

Then someone suggested returning to London by train. We brightened up at the prospect. It was the answer to all of our problems. We leaped on our cycles and pedalled the remaining miles into Brighton in good spirits, arriving exhausted, but with some optimism.

We were ravenous when we reached the station. They told us it was another hour before the London train, so we looked for a restaurant. A greasy spoon preferably. We could only find a moderately posh one. Jack was unhappy about going in wearing indigo shorts, while Frank and I were equally unhappy at the prospect of being seen with such a strangely attired person, said shorts displaying an almost luminescent quality in the fading light.

Jack expressed bitterness at having made such a sartorial gaffe and blamed us for not also having naked legs. He added that the restaurant probably had dress rules and would throw him out. Ever helpful, we suggested he take his bike in with him to reinforce his claim to being a bon-fide cyclist, rather than a weirdo.

In the event, the staff took no notice and Jack hid his legs and shorts under the tablecloth at a corner table. An ordinary, but overpriced, meal followed. After paying for it, we then had to pool resources to cover the train fare, for ourselves and bikes, to Streatham station. The plan was to leave the bikes at my house—just a stones-throw from the station— and let Jack and Frank complete their journey home by London Bus.

It was late by the time we reached my house. Frank went home immediately after dropping off his bike, but Jack hung around looking glum. He then confessed he couldn't face the late bus to Upper Norwood wearing indigo shorts. There were usually a few drunks on it and if they saw him, he was doomed.

He slept on our settee that night.

Chapter 23: Private Water.

In the summer of 1956, on what promised to be a fine day, my friends had arranged a fishing trip to the river Wey, near Byfleet. It was the dawn of a new era for us. Gone were the exhausting cycle rides with tackle and rods strapped to our backs. Pete, another friend from the model aircraft club, had bought a car.

The vehicle was a 1934 Standard Little Nine. It had a side-valve engine that throbbed out a mighty 22bhp. Impressive in a lawnmower perhaps? However, with four people inside a car it could barely pull *itself* along, let alone overtake anything.

It had bald tyres, a leaky radiator and left a smokescreen in its wake. Pete was proud of his vehicle, in spite of its shortcomings. For the rest of us it was a great deal better than cycling with rods strapped to our backs, and more comfortable than my motorbike.

The sun had only just risen when I cycled from Streatham to Mitcham to join Dusty and Pete at Brian's house. We then piled into the car in high spirits, somehow finding room for our tackle boxes on our laps, with the rods sticking out of the sunshine roof.

Any journey with a motor car was an adventure in those days. There was always the possibility of mechanical failure, or even being prosecuted for some document oversight. But we were optimistic to the point of recklessness.

The old car ran like a dream, although not a particularly vivid one. It took us to our destination on empty roads and relished the challenge of overtaking the odd milk float. Actually succeeding a couple of times when we were going downhill.

We fished in a secluded spot near a bend in the river, the warm, sultry morning dreaming along to a sweltering mid-day, without us catching a single fish. We cooked a primitive lunch on our spirit stove and settled for an afternoon of peace and tranquillity.

The cooling embrace of the river beckoned those of us who could swim, so Pete and I stripped off and slithered over the reeds into the dubious green-brown water. We found it surprisingly cold. We headed off around the bend at a fast crawl, enjoying the coolness of the water and the exercise. However, our pleasure was interrupted, and the peace shattered, by a shrill voice.

"I thay! Go away… Thith ith pwivate water," it shrieked.

At the river's edge was a chunky girl of about sixteen. She was wearing a bright pink sundress, somehow giving the impression of a large blancmange looking down its nose at us. Behind her was a long strip of perfect lawn, hanging, like a badly chosen tie, from an impressive white stucco house.

We stopped swimming and held our position by treading water a few yards away from her. We were attempting to process, in our minds, what she was trying to tell us.

Upon realizing there was some hostility in her demeanour we shouted, with good humour, "You don't own the water we're swimming in, because it has only just arrived from further upstream. We are quite happy here and intend to stay for a while—why don't you stwip off and join us?"

The chublet, in high dudgeon, turned towards the house, stamped her foot, and piped, "Papa. Papa, wude boys in the wiver."

A figure detached itself from a deckchair and came gangling towards us. He looked like a cross between Charles Hawtry and Kenneth Williams. The raucous music of an Ealing Comedy could almost be imagined playing in the distance.

"Don't y' know you're twespassing. This part of the wivver is pwivate!" he shrieked in a falsetto voice.

We gaped in amazement. How could this puny, effete creature have fathered such a sturdy little pink hoyden? A feeling of sympathy started to invade our mirth, *could* such speech affectations be inherited? Or did they just practice until they got it right?

A woman, who we assumed to be the mother, then joined the unlikely duo. She was quite gorgeous and spoke normally, but with a plummy accent. She assumed a more conciliatory tone and seemed of the opinion that having a pair of athletic, naked, eighteen-year-old lads floating around at the bottom of her garden was more of an asset than a threat.

Although tempted to prolong our jolly sport, and starting to fancy the mother like mad, we feared they might start talking about their 'riparian rights.' Attempts to use more such words beginning with 'R' could cause them embarrassment and make us laugh until we drowned.

We were a little embarrassed ourselves, at our nakedness—we had not planned on chatting to any girls and the water was fairly clear in this part of the river. The chance we were committing a public decency offence was not far from our minds. The pink chublet had her hands over her eyes, but we could see she was looking at us from between her fingers.

The current was fairly strong as we reluctantly took our leave of them and allowed ourselves to drift back to our companions. We gave a friendly wave as we disappeared from their view, just to show there was no ill feeling on our part.

We lay on the bank dozing until six o'clock. Pub opening time was then upon us, no fish had been caught, and it was time to leave.

We returned to the car to find a flat tyre, and there was no jack in the toolbox. However, three of us managed to lift the car while the fourth bolted on a spare wheel that had a tyre on it so bald it was showing canvas. We badly needed to wash our hands after manhandling the dirty old car, and even dirtier spare wheel. So, we stopped in a likely pub near Morden. After cleaning ourselves up, and over refreshing glasses of lager and lime, we discussed the fascinating encounter Pete and I had on the river.

"You could well have wandered on to a film set. They couldn't have been real people, could they?" Dusty said, after Pete, and I had re-performed the encounter pantomime fashion—but with our shirts and trousers on.

"Probably actors escaped from Shepperton Studio. They're always letting them out," I suggested. This area of Surrey was strangely infested with actors and bit part players with loud, posh, voices. They could be heard braying in the saloon bars of many local pubs.

"Still, they can be a laugh at times, and often buy drinks all-round if they land a good part," Dusty said in their defence.

We all agreed the encounter had made the day interesting. It had been bloody hot, and the fish certainly hadn't performed for us.

Chapter 24: Four Wheels

September 1957. I was nineteen years old, and the family had moved down from London to the Kent market town of Ashford.

I was continuing my electrical engineering training at a local factory and things were looking settled. All I needed was a car. I had a motorcycle and a bicycle, but was not looking forward to winter. No longer did I have the convenient and regular services of the London transport buses when the weather was bad.

There had been an unfortunate mishap with my current motorbike—A KTT Velocette. It was a mid-1930s, TT racing machine and a more unsuitable vehicle for going to and from work would be difficult to find. I managed to bend the crankshaft when the dynamo fell off, jamming between the road and the engine sprocket. As the accident progressed the machine had, as usual, leapt in the air casting me into the gutter, while the bike clattered on its side to the centre of the road. I had become quite used to this sort of thing happening.

The Velocette would have been very expensive to repair as it was such a rare machine. I was not aware just how rare it was at the time and how valuable. Foolishly, with total lack of foresight, I sold it for next to nothing. Sixty years later I found out it had been sent to the US.

My uncle and aunt, who lived a few miles north of Ashford in Challock had a 1933 Standard Big 9

Saloon languishing in a shed. It was surplus to requirements, since my uncle had bought a more modern car. He had owned it from almost new, having bought it from a vicar, so the car even had a tenuous link with God. Impeccable pedigree for such a vehicle. He was prepared to accept £35 for it. The Standard had been laid up during the war, and afterwards had mainly been used for trips into Ashford for haircuts. Consequently, it was in pretty good nick for its age and had been christened 'The Blue Monster.'

As it was during the Suez crisis, petrol was rationed and driving tests had been discontinued. The government had, therefore, lifted the restriction on learners driving without a qualified driver alongside them. Interesting times.

The relaxation of rules meant that in spite of never having driven a car before, I could attach 'L' plates and drive it the eight miles home, spreading terror through the centre of Ashford on the way. I was game for this, but first it meant finding out how to change gear and make the semaphore indicators work.

Uncle gave me a half-hour lesson on the Challock Leas, opposite his smallholding. I found it pretty easy and emerged out on to the Canterbury Road as an experienced and fully trained driver. I set off for the other side of Ashford with the sort of confidence only the young and inexperienced can conjure up.

I arrived home without hitting anything important, although horns were sounded and fists shaken at me a couple of times. Having ridden a motorcycle for three years probably gave me some road sense and saved many from a messy death during this epic eight-mile drive.

Although a very sound motor—capable of reliably taking me to any pub I wanted to visit—I was young and enthusiastic and thought the car needed jazzing up. I had seen pictures of similar-shaped cars built by Americans, with V8 engines and lots of chrome. I wanted to turn it into something like that. Mother made me some smart seat covers, and I painted the engine red to give the impression of power. Not as much power as a V8 engine would have given, but the girls I hoped to impress were unlikely to know that. More instrumentation was needed to make the sparse dashboard look more technical. So, to this end, I fitted a huge temperature gauge from a WW2 Mosquito aircraft. Such desirable ex WD goodies were available for a few pence from surplus stores. From the same source a switch panel was fitted, with six switches—only one of which was connected to anything. I also fitted an extra fuse panel in the engine compartment, just in case I wanted to wire in more accessories.

This was an impoverished apprentice's idea of pimping up a car in 1957. The Standard Big Nine's maximum speed was still only an unsafe forty-five miles an hour.

With the coming of winter, the horrors of owning an old car in the 50s was brought home to me. With the first hard frost of the year I would be woken in the morning by a familiar noise from every street. I can only describe it as a laborious whirr-whirr-whirr, gradually slowing to a whir... whir... click! The depressing sound of a car battery going flat after failing to start the car. You would then hear the rattle of a car bonnet being opened followed by the loud clattering of a starting handle being inserted and turned. The racket this made caused any further sleep to be impossible.

The dreaded frosty morning car starting ritual had begun. For those who could afford it, the problems could be eased by changing to a winter grade oil, and possibly buying a new battery. It was also advisable to add antifreeze to the cooling system to avoid the engine freezing and being damaged. This could be a big expense and often resulted in an old car being scrapped. The downside of antifreeze, apart from the expense, was it exposed any weakness in the cooling system and could all drain away during the night.

A little paraffin heater to hang under the bonnet, or place under the sump was another way of stopping the engine from freezing—again, if you could afford it. For those who didn't have the money to spend, getting up earlier was advisable. One had to drain the radiator at night, and re-fill with warm water the following morning. The car would usually start easily after this, but if really cold the radiator could freeze up as you drove along. There was an accessory called a Radiator Muff available, and if you were lucky your car would have one. Failing that, a piece of cardboard blocking off the lower part of the radiator would usually prevent freezing.

Everyone would be driving in gloves and an overcoat because few cars had heaters in those days, and you also had to stop frequently to clear any frost build-up on the windscreen. I found winter driving to be quite an adventure.

It was February 1958 before the Suez crisis and petrol rationing ended. Driving tests resumed and I was no longer allowed to drive on my own, needing to have a qualified driver with me. My father had been useful for this, but he could give little advice on driving having never driven a car himself. He had owned a small motorcycle in 1932 when they had issued him with a licence to drive almost anything. He later bought a car and became a public nuisance.

I had a few lessons from a Mr Wilson's driving School, in Ashford, at £0 17s 6p an hour. Eventually I passed my test in Folkestone in early April. The world was now my oyster. I had a great summer exploring Kent in the Blue Monster. I got to visit all the pubs I had always wanted to try, and even drove up to London to spend a weekend with my old friends.

I was to own another ten pre-WW2 cars before I settled down to Marriage, and a sensible post-war VW Beetle. My particular favourites of the older cars was a 1935 Vauxhall fourteen six coupe, and the stately and comfortable 1938 Rover sixteen I courted my wife in.

Twenty years later I bought a 1932 Austin 10/4 as a restoration project. After restoring it I used it for thirty-five years as a second car. I have tried to have at least one pre-war car or motorcycle on the road ever since.

Chapter 25: Grass Track Racing

In 1958 I was running around in a 1947 Austin 8 van. It was a nice shade of blue and you could hardly see the writing on the side. The painted-over lettering suggested it had previously been used for transporting haberdashery. A rub down with abrasive and another coat of paint would have completely hidden its humble origins, but I wasn't bothered. It was quite smart, for me, and the first post-WW2 vehicle I owned, before returning, again, to the pre-war variety.

I struck up a friendship with Len, a chap who had just joined the firm I was working for. He was building a grass- racing motorcycle in his shed and would need transport to various racing venues. It would just fit in my van. But he had to finish building the bike and get it running first.

The fact that he had never ridden a motorcycle before in his life would not, he hoped, impact his performance too much when it came to his first race.

It took some work to eventually get it running, which was down to me, because he wasn't much of a mechanic either. I remember us pushing it up and down the lane to try and get the engine to fire. It was having none of it until I remembered the points should be set to open before the piston reached top dead centre, rather than after. I apologise for the boring mechanical details, I shall endeavour not to use any more of them.

We reset the points, Len leaped aboard, and I pushed. It started instantly, carrying Len up the lane, across the road, and into a bank at the other side. We had power and had, somehow, appeased the Gods of Internal Combustion. Next, we had to teach Len to use the handbrake lever. But first, up to The Plough in Smeeth to celebrate our brilliance with a Mackeson's or two.

We took the bike to a nearby field and practiced dashing around, flat out—or almost. Len could now ride—after a fashion—and couldn't wait to win his first race. Our first race meeting was at Barham. It was a sort of kidney-shaped track on the side of a hill, just a few miles from Lydden. Len went out in high spirits expecting great things of the bike. To be truthful Len had sourced a pretty good, well-tuned 250 JAP engine from a friend, but the telescopic forks were not man enough. They seemed to flex at every bump.

Len fell off in practice. Not discouraged he tried again… and fell off again. He did not have the years of practice I had in falling off bikes. It showed in the way he was began limping.

Practice was over and the first race was due. Len gave me his helmet and told me I could go out in his place. He needed more practice before he felt ready to mix it with the others. They wouldn't notice it wasn't him riding because in grass-track racing one idiot looked pretty much the same as any other. The first race was for 250cc machines only. So theoretically, no one would have a machine much more powerful than the one I was riding. On the other hand, I had not had any practice and it was my first ever motorcycle race. The starting flag was up almost before I realized it and taking a handful of throttle I dashed towards the first bend. When I reached it, I found I was in the lead.

Now that *was* terrifying. I had visions of falling off and all the rest riding over me, so I throttled back and let a few overtake me. I eventually finished well down the field.

Well, that was exciting. I couldn't wait for the next race, but those front forks were giving me cause for concern. They did not like bumps and nearly had me off a couple of times.

The next race was an unlimited class. A race where most of the machines would be more powerful than the bike I was riding. I moved off cautiously, making sure I was not too far up in the first bend. I wasn't. In fact, one bike overtook me and I found myself in last place. I gritted my teeth and wound up the throttle. I was starting to make up ground, until I hit a bump and the front forks twisted. I hit the ground, hard, and the bike cartwheeled away across the track. I was winded and dizzy. Trying to get to my feet, I realised how far I had dropped behind when the leaders came around on the second lap. I had to roll into a ball to avoid being hit.

Dragging myself off the track I was relieved to see Marshalls dragging the bike off. They asked if I needed help to get to the St John's Ambulance van. No way. They would want my name and competition certificate number. Best I get back to Len, and my own van, then slip off home. Len was glumly examining the damage to the bike. It mainly consisted of a broken fuel tank bracket.

"Hardly a scratch, whereas I'm crippled for life," I told him, as I struggled to walk on a leg that was stiff and painful.

It turned out to be an uncomfortable journey home. I tried not to change gear too much because my left leg was agony to use. This, with an eight-horsepower engine, three passengers, and a motorcycle, was not easy. It turned out I had badly bruised the bone on my left thigh and was hobbling about for weeks before it eased off.

Enthusiasm then waned for grass track racing. Len started to spend more time with his girlfriend and I had a new set of friends in Tenterden.

The part of my leg that had the knock had a strange numb feeling after that. Thirty-eight years later I had to have some sort of growth removed from it.

I never had the desire to race motorcycles again, although it didn't dampen my enthusiasm for owning them. Just after the operation to remove the growth, I retook my motorcycle test in order to use the Ariel square four I had just restored.

Chapter 26: Tractor

Tollgate Nurseries was up and running well by 1950, and all the greenhouses necessary at that time had been built. There were at least ten large greenhouses and dozens of cold frames producing tomatoes, cucumbers, and various flowers for market. There were three 'smallish' fields not under glass that needed cultivating to grow daffodils, tulips, chrysanthemums and a couple of other flowers that would tolerate being grown outside.

The dreadful two-wheeled 'Iron horse' tractor had accompanied them in their move from their previous nursery business in Tenterden at West Cross. However, the task of cultivating so much land with this machine was to prove exhausting and almost futile. They needed a tractor.

The only one immediately available, and suitable for such a task, was a pre-war Fordson Standard tractor.

The Fordson had been one of the most widely used pieces of farm machinery for many years. It also gave great service as a towing vehicle for the RAF during the war. It was still ideal though, as a general workhorse for a small farm. It was the agricultural version, and even shared some components with the Model 'T' Ford car. The paintwork had evolved into a shade of ferrous oxide and the vehicle had those cleated iron wheels that left permanent marks on tarmac roads throughout the countryside, endearing themselves to every council's road repair department.

The crude and brutal engine was started by swinging a handle. It would spring into life easily and with little effort when new, often on the first attempt. However, with the ravages of age and wear on the pistons and cylinders, strong men would be known to weep after a couple of hours of it failing to start.

The particular weakness of my grandfather's tractor was the magneto... the device that gives the plugs their spark. The engine would start only if you were lucky, and if damp hadn't entered the magneto over the winter months.

In the winter, unless the tractor was in regular use and kept under cover, the magneto would suck up moisture and refuse to spark. It was best to remove it and keep it in the airing cupboard until needed. The extra work involved doing this was negligible compared with blistering your hands by swinging the starting handle for ages and then having to remove the magneto and dry it out anyway.

The unloved iron horse found itself parked in the long grass alongside the pond, rusting gently away. It was to be only used in the direst emergences, if absolutely nothing else was available. No one in the world felt any fondness for it as the poor brute was the repository of too many bad memories.

The Fordson tractor had one of those bouncy cast iron seats mounted on a leaf spring—almost as good as a fairground ride to a youngster—and it sported two fuel tanks. A small one for petrol that was used to start the engine, then a tap would switch a second one to the cheaper paraffin or TVO when the manifolds were hot enough to vaporize it. The vehicle was a crude device by modern standards, but built to last almost forever if looked after. Which they rarely were.

On past visits, when I was younger, the tractor had just been something to bounce up and down on. It was always parked in the second of the three fields.

There were a couple of times I had seen it used while I was there on holiday. I would watch Uncle Horace with his hands blistered and sweat pouring off him, as he tried to induce it to start. The choice of words to use in the process seemed particularly important to the likelihood of success—like finding the right formula for a magic spell. My uncle's use of obscenities almost became poetic. I never heard him swear at any other time.

I had become interested in machinery as the years went by, my uncle having explained to me, in expert detail, how the internal combustion engine worked. He had always wanted to be an engineer himself, but had followed the family business and become a flower grower. Something he regretted.

I had already passed through the motorcycle stage, where I had taught myself how to pull engines apart and, in many cases, actually put them back together again, before graduating to my first car and passing my driving test. I loved all mechanical things, but only as a hobby. The day job involved electronics, and, I hoped, management eventually.

The tractor interested me strangely. I knew I had to drive it or my education would not be complete. There was a patch of ground designated for tulips in the second field, and it needed the attention of the harrow. I insisted I was just the man to do it because I had been getting a great deal of experience of using a starting handle on my own car. Grandfather warned me my uncle had almost given up trying to start the tractor and cheerfully wished me luck.

I attacked the handle with enthusiasm, getting the engine to fire the second time. Encouraged, I cranked away for about ten minutes, only stopping when I was exhausted and my hands were starting to blister. The thing was obviously the mechanical version of a recalcitrant mule. I thought I might have just the one more attempt before going to grandfather and admitting defeat.

It started.

The engine sounded rough, but I released the clutch and it trundled off down the field nicely leaving a strip of freshly harrowed earth behind it. I soon got hang of harrowing and nearly half the field was done before the tractor's engine note changed. It gave a throaty cough and stopped in the middle of the field.

I jumped down and checked the fuel tank. There was still plenty in there. I gave the handle a couple of swings, but there was something about the feel of the engine that told me its problem was not trivial.

There were many attempts to revive it, both by myself and my uncle. It remained dead though. It was as if it knew it had done enough in this life and was anxious to get to the foundry and be resurrected as something more adventurous. The tractor had had a long career, spanning possibly thirty years, before taking its last breath in the idyllic setting of a little field on the edge of the Romney Marsh.

It occurred to me I might resurrect the old iron horse to get the job finished, but grandfather made arrangements with a neighbouring farm to do the small amount of tractor work needed at the nurseries. Most of the attention was now on the greenhouses, and one of the fields was leased to a neighbour.

Whenever I see a vintage Fordson tractor ploughing at one of the country shows, or rusting sadly in pub gardens with children playing on it, I can almost feel the blisters on the palms of my hands again and even smell the sweat and paraffin.

However, I'm glad I got the chance to drive one while they were still in everyday use. It was the last piece of farm work I was ever to do.

Chapter 27: The Triangle

I had planned to fish Dengemarsh that evening with my friend Dave. We had been hoping to fish until the small hours and take advantage of the unusually good run of cod that year. I had assured my neighbours they were in for a treat when I came home laden with codling and whiting. In those days I shared the catch around, because no one had a freezer and I don't like wasting good fish.

Dave dropped out with flu at the last moment, so I was on my own.

It was late September in nineteen sixty-one, and in those days you could set your watch by the arrival of codling and channel whiting on the first day of the month. The weather was absolutely still. No wind at all, but a dank and heavy mist shrouded the marsh, making driving difficult as the visibility was down to less than fifty yards in places.

I drove from Ashford in my old Vauxhall DX, with the windscreen open to give better visibility in the swirling mist. There was a spot between the offside wing and headlamp where I could just make out the white line in the road. I pulled my old naval duffel coat hood up to avoid my ears getting frostbite, but the mist was getting into my lungs. It was going to be cold and damp that night, but I was young and could take that sort of thing then. What I dreaded most was driving along the potholed Dengemarsh track for a couple of miles, with no white line to follow and deep dykes on either side.

I needed to get some rest before the long night's fishing, but had spent lunchtime in the pub, carousing with a jolly bunch of friends. I had some time to use up before the bait diggers delivered the day's haul. I sat dozing in the car outside the tackle shop.

As I left the tackle shop packing three score of slithies into my bait bag, the mist seemed to thicken and a decrepit old fellow, possibly a retired filleter, appeared out of the gloom. A skinny hand shot out and vice-like, grabbed my wrist.

"You'll not have slithies in that bag and be fishing the Denge, would you, young sir?" he asked in old Marsh-talk, his voice crackling with age.

I shook myself free and affirmed this was indeed the case. He motioned me to sit with him on a low wall. Then proceeded to recount a tale. A tale that made my hair stand out like the spines on a fretful porpentine, as Shakespeare might have said.

"It was like this, young sir," he said, breathing stale tobacco smoke into my face, and in his strange patois, sounding part old Kentish, and part didicoi, he continued:

"I'd been down to the muddy flats, where I dug a hundred prime slithies, and sunned them for three matins til they were middlin' rancid." At this point I interrupted him to point out the present shortage of slithies, and suggest that the power station they were starting to build was to blame. He then grabbed me by the shoulders, looked straight into my face with his troubled, rheumy old eyes, and said forcefully, "Hear me out young sir, I beg you, or you may live to regret it!"

Alarmed by his manner I bade him continue, as I wished to hear his story. He refilled his pipe, scratched his gonads and continued. "I biked along the gnarly road from Lydd, with no light save an old hurricane lantern. It were deathly quiet, not even woollies bleatin' in the fields when I arrived. I waved to the coastguard as he locked the lookout post and went home for the night. Then, after parking my bike against the wall I carried my gear up to the triangle."

"That's where I intend to fish tonight," I told him.

"More fool you, if you'll not mind me saying so, young sir."

"Is there some reason I shouldn't?" I asked, feeling thoroughly alarmed.

"Just hear me out sir and make your own judgement. As I set up my old cane rod and cast out a knot of slithies, the moon went behind a cloud and it were black as a vole's weskit. It was like being drownded' in a slurry tank. Lookin,' toward the slapple of the surf, all I could see were dozens of evil little eyes peering at me, wikkid like. Fair spooked I was. I turned to me lantern and it went out. As if the wind had blown it, but there wasn't no wind. As I felt for me matches, I heard the scrunchel of the pebbles. Like marching' feet it was. I swear the eyes were growing larger and closer."

"Whatever were they?" I interrupted, becoming more than a little spooked myself.

"Who knows, young sir. Who knows what may be abroad on that desolate, scareful beach? All I know is, I hirpled off up the shingle, squittering and yodelling like a demented cackler. The missus was fair put out by the manky state of me trews, when I arrived, fair knakkled, at me cottage."

With his story finished, he got up from the wall and seemed to dissolve into the mist.

There was a rapping on the window of the car, and I jumped like I had been stung by a wasp. I wound down the window and it was the owner of the bait shop. He told me he was about to close but had kept back three score of slithies for me. This was strange, because I was sure I already had the slithies when I had started to talk to the old bloke.

Feeling very shaken I enquired if he had seen me talking to an old filleter, and described the old fellow of my dream. If indeed it had been a dream.

"You were fast asleep in the car the last couple of hours and didn't move, but the fellow you mention sounds like old Agony Pope," the bait vendor said quietly and nervously.

Then he beckoned me to come closer and spoke in a low, yet urgent voice. "Old Agony Pope's been dead these last fifteen years. Found washed up on Denge beach clutching a broken fishing rod. At the inquest they said he hadn't drownded. Because there weren't no water in his lungs. Most folk say he was frightened to death."

That night I fished the east side of Dungey point, caught sod-all, but would never again fish Dengemarsh Beach after nightfall.

Chapter 28: The Boat With No Name

I first became involved with boat fishing in the mid nineteen-sixties. Ticking off yet another type of transport on my list. I bought a half-share in a 12ft sailing dinghy that had been tragically parted from its mast at some stage. My friend Brian already owned the other half of the boat. A few years previously he had come down from Mitcham to stay the weekend with me, met a girl and married. He now lived in an idyllic little village in the weald.

As wind propulsion was no longer available to the boat, a small single cylinder outboard engine called the Century 100 Plus, was attached to the stern. The plus part was very important because it meant it was equipped with a clutch. Yet another fascinating piece of machinery for me to play with.

The hull was built of marine ply which could be somewhat fragile. It was not advisable to stamp about too much in the bilges. There was a story going about where an angler, upon catching a large conger from a similar marine ply boat, became so concerned at its threatening and unruly behaviour that he stamped on the creature's head, hoping to discourage it. His foot went right through the bottom of the boat causing it to sink beneath him. This thoroughly ruined his day's fishing and the conger escaped with little worse than a headache.

Such hazards were not for people like us with family responsibilities. We resolved to make the boat sturdy and unsinkable. We would sheath it in fibreglass, then add buoyancy by way of dozens of empty plastic bottles fastened to the inside of the hull. This major feat of boatbuilding was carried out in a small barn in the sleepy village of Frittenden, where The Bell Inn was close enough to provide the sustenance needed for such tasks.

The day dawned when the boat was ready to launch and commence sea trials. Try as I may, I cannot recollect us naming the boat. We will refer to it henceforth, as the *Boat with No Name.* We were relieved that, in spite of additions, it was still light enough for the two of us to lift on to the trailer. The trailer was an interesting beast in itself, having been constructed from an old bedstead with the front suspension units from two Vespa scooters. The whole thing was going to be towed behind Brian's little Austin A30 car.

Dengemarsh was the chosen venue to wet the new fibreglass hull. At that time, it was the nearest you could get to the sea from a road. However, there was still fifteen yards of shingle to manhandle the boat across, but we were young and fit, and laughed at such inconveniences.

We did not respect the sea enough, having no idea of the danger we were to put ourselves in. I was a strong swimmer and thought that enough.

Brian, although he couldn't swim, had faith in his lifejacket and private school education. He was usually able to provide the voice of reason and caution, as well as a degree of buoyancy if needed.

When I look back, I shudder at our recklessness. By then we were both married with young families. We must have been mad. Somehow, we are both still here though.

To get back to the Dengemarsh epic. It was low tide when we dragged the boat across the shingle and launched it. We negotiated the inshore breakers without incident and the motor started at the first pull. We were at sea. All we needed was a beaver sitting on the prow making lace, and we could have been hunting Snarks.

"This is the life!" Brian shouted above the phut-phut of the engine. Strangely enough on all subsequent trips, one or the other of us would shout that.

We steamed off around the point in high spirits, dropping anchor at what seemed a good place. We then cast out our lines seeking to decimate the sea-life below us. A few dab, pouting, and a couple of nice channel whiting fell victim to our efforts before we noticed the sea nearby boiling with tiny baitfish. I was about to meet my first shoal of mackerel.

Sets of feathers were hurriedly fastened to our lines, which were then lowered and jigged about just below the boat. The mackerel came in five at a time, until we were both exhausted and feared the weight of them may sink the boat. We then reluctantly pulled in our lines, upped anchor, and headed back for Dengemarsh beach.

On this first occasion we were lucky, the tide was fairly low and we managed to beach the boat without the rear end of it sinking as the prow hit the shingle. On higher tides there was a steep shingle bank to beach the boat on. The one of us in the stern clutching the motor would not only find himself up to the waist in water but having to suffer the frustration of watching our catch float away. This was to happen on a couple of occasions, until we learned not to come in at high tide. However, if the weather blew up rough there was no other option.

Not yet having freezers at home, we gave surplus fish away or sold them for a few coppers to holidaymakers on the beach. We never took home more than we, or our family and neighbours, were likely to need.

This was the first of many successful fishing trips in the *Boat with No Name*. The best ever took place on a frosty morning on November fifth, nineteen sixty-seven—a date forever engraved on our memories.

We left Brian's house at around seven in the morning. We were fishing from the slipway at St Mary's Bay, but first had to visit Marnie's tackle shop in New Romney, for bait.

At last, we had discovered that using slipways was easier than dragging the boat across shingle and then being swamped if we returned at high tide. The dangers of fishing Dengemarsh were no longer worth facing.

We unhitched the boat, and between us trundled it down the slipway on to the sand. The tide was halfway out, but no matter. We unloaded the boat at the water's edge and by the time we had taken the trailer somewhere safe, we would return to find the boat ready to float off. Easy-peasy compared with dragging it up and down shingle.

The sea was perfectly calm on that day. The frost had gone off and it was almost warm. We had only managed to get a couple of score of lug worm but that many were usually sufficient for a morning's fishing. *This* morning was going to be different though.

The sport started with a double figure cod. Then we continued to catch decent cod and good-sized channel whiting for the next two hours. As we started to run out of bait, we were reduced to finding small pieces on the deck, and even dragging mangled worms from the fish's throats. The seabed must have been alive with fish. Fortunately, the bait ran out completely before the weight of the fish sank the boat.

We now had an embarrassment of fish. Some 2 cwt of them. We could usually get rid of our surplus catch with no problem amongst friends and relatives, but we'd never had this many at one time before, presenting us with a unique challenge. In those days there was no talk of sustainability and only taking what you need, but at least we never threw anything away. We detoured through Tenterden on the way home, handing out fish left and right to anyone we knew. We had no bags to put them in, so several people were seen wandering down Tenterden High Street clutching a cod by the tail. Not a common sight in that fair town.

There were many more adventures with the nameless craft. Once, we tried our hand at night fishing in Dover Harbour with our efforts illuminated by a Tilley Lamp mounted on a pole. We were chased off by an angry fellow in a peaked cap commanding the harbour patrol boat. He claimed we had wandered across the shipping lane and should not have been boating in the harbour at night anyway.

We caught one eel that night, which was found in the bottom of the boat a couple of days later. Still perky, as eels tend to be, and looking for adventure. We had adventures a'plenty for such a creature.

It first had a ride in a bucket to my aunt and uncle in Challock, where Uncle suggested it be set free in the swimming pool to help keep it clean through the coming winter. It was then forgotten until the spring pool-cleaning ritual, where we all used to scrub it out for the coming summer. Absolute panic ensued when its slightly larger serpentine presence became evident around people's feet.

In the next stage of its adventures, it was again given a ride in a bucket to a beautiful lake at Eastwell Park. There it was abandoned to find its own way to the Sargasso Sea where eels are ultimately known to head. No doubt it had many more adventures on the way.

Brian eventually bought himself a better boat, and I became sole owner of the *Boat with No Name*. Just the boat, not the outboard motor.

There were to be a couple of interesting, bordering on disastrous, trips with it before it 'really had to go'.

Chapter 29: Selling the Boat With No Name

A British Anzani outboard motor, retrieved from a lorry load of rubbish on the way to the refuse tip, was given to me free of charge by a friend, who thought I may have a use for it.

I found it to be in good condition and nowhere near as old as the one we had been using. However, there was no way I could use it at sea until I had done a very careful overhaul to establish why it had been thrown away.

Meanwhile, a neighbour suggested a trip out from Dengemarsh using my boat. His own boat was too heavy to drag across the shingle but we could use his outboard. This sounded like a good scheme. I had already forgotten how dangerous it was there.

I had a feeling of foreboding upon realizing the motor we were using was a Sea Bee. Nice for pottering around in ponds, but for seagoing they did not have a good reputation. My worst fears were realized when it packed up a quarter of a mile from shore, resisting all efforts to restart it. We always carried a pair of oars for such emergencies, and they were pressed into service, but a quarter mile with an offshore wind is a long way to row—as we found out.

We were totally exhausted, having drifted almost as far as a place called Galloways, on the military firing range, by the time we touched shore. We then had our first piece of luck, finding ourselves only a hundred yards from a piece of military road.

We had a long trudge back to Dengemarsh to collect the car from the coastguard post. The coastguard greeted us with relief, saying he had watched us every inch of our epic rowing adventure and missed his lunch as a result.

I started looking for a wannabee seafarer with a few spare shekels in his pocket to take the craft off my hands before I ended up drowned. However, the *Boat with No Name*'s last, and biggest adventure was yet to come. There was a chap at work. A thirtyish single guy, known as 'H,' who was always looking for adventure. He found it mainly on one-armed bandits down at the Bowling Centre.

I suggested that a seafaring life (on a limited scale,) was what he may have been looking for. I told myself it might well be less expensive than his Bandit habit. All he needed was a small boat, and I was the man to supply it.

He then, mercilessly, beat me down on the asking price until I was almost giving it away. Then wanted a test run to make sure it did not suffer from shipworm and was likely to sink. I made a mental note never to become a professional boat seller. I was not good at it.

The day of the test run was windy and overcast. A force six gale was forecast in the estuary. Seeing his disappointment at this news, I suggested a trip to Rye Harbour, where we could run up and down the river Rother. It should be sheltered there with little chance of mishap.

We left my house in an optimistic mood and headed across the marsh to Rye. We were then in darkest Sussex where I had had no seafaring experience. Launching in a stiff current, we headed towards the harbour mouth, hoping to go far enough to see the state of the sea off Camber Sands. It was calm and sheltered, but with a slight swell. We agreed we may be able to do a spot of fishing there.

We then left the safety of the harbour arm. Not a smart thing to do in retrospect, especially when H mentioned he couldn't swim and wasn't wearing a life jacket.

I made him put one on straight away. I can't recall why he wasn't wearing one in the first place — I must have thought he was wearing an inflatable one. It is over fifty years ago now.

We were fishing happily, carefully keeping an eye on the swell, when the freak wave came on us unexpectedly. It broke over us and caused us to ship quite a lot of water. 'Lucky to get away with that,' I thought, and started to bail out the water. Another, even bigger, wave then arrived, and flipped us upside down.

My world went green. I don't know why because from the surface the water was brown. I found myself beneath the boat and desperately striking out for the surface.

I came up alongside the capsized hull and all I could think of was H, probably somewhere beneath me and drowning. How would I explain it to his mates at work? I hadn't meant this to happen.

To my great relief he popped up coughing and spluttering, alongside me. Grabbing him I dragged him on to the upturned boat. He was, fortunately, not a large man. We tried to make ourselves comfortable and wait for help to arrive. Someone must have seen us, surely. If not, the tide was dropping fast and in a short while we would be able to walk to safety.

Unbelievably, a larger angling boat we had seen fishing nearby, came alongside. On a falling tide there was very little water for a boat of that size, and the skipper must have had nerves of steel. We scrambled aboard and they took us back to the harbour.

We both had a change of clothing in the car, but needed to get dry, and change somewhere warm. The posh yacht club changing rooms came to our rescue after a kind soul allowed us in. Then some creep came along and asked for proof of membership. There was a row between the two. However, while the row was going on, we dried ourselves and got changed, thanking them kindly as we left. A week later, I found I had caught a verruca — the only one I ever had in my life.

We drove some three miles to Camber sands to find the boat high and dry on a sandbank. Exactly where we had left it because there had been no time to pull up the anchor. All our gear was scattered around on the sand.

For some reason, H had brought his expensive camera and binoculars with him. Both were now half buried in the sand. Finding my fishing rod, I reeled it in to find I had caught an excellent whiting, but H did not offer any congratulations on this fact. I was still admiring the fish, when, from nowhere, we found ourselves surrounded by inshore lifeboatmen.

Apparently, there had been a report of an upturned boat and people clinging to the bottom. These men had come along to collect the bodies, being quite chipper to find us alive and unharmed. They were a splendid bunch of chaps. They turned the boat upright and towed it back to the harbour for us. We then met them back at the lifeboat station where they broke out the rum.

We gave them a donation—at least H did—for rescuing the boat. Quite right too. If he hadn't wanted to buy it and have a demonstration none of this would have happened. Any money I had was still in my soaked back pocket, somewhere in the car. I did send them an envelope a couple of days later.

On the way home H dried his money on the dashboard. I had little doubt that none of it would come my way. He was surprisingly relaxed about the whole episode, although he'd lost his enthusiasm for seafaring.

All was not lost. After doing an overhaul and washing the sand and barnacles out of the outboard motor, it started instantly. The boat itself, although a bit scraped, was still useable. I advertised it locally and the first person to answer the advert bought it for a better price than I had previously hoped for. He didn't want a demonstration of its capabilities, and I didn't offer one.

It was to be over ten years before I would own a boat again. But that is another story.

Chapter 30: The Herne Bay Car and Boating Years

In 1979 we bought a three-story Victorian pile in Herne Bay. It had seven bedrooms, allowing room for my ailing in-laws, and lots of space for our boys to grow up in. It was a few hundred yards from the sea and I must confess, fishing and boating were not far from my thoughts when we bought it.

Finding the time to fish was going be a problem. I had a demanding job that required frequent foreign and domestic travel. On the plus side though I now lived only half a mile from my office.

One of the local Angling Clubs had a dinghy festival attracting hundreds of entrants each year. I had entered it once with Brian when I had lived in Ashford. Although we had brought his boat with us, for some reason we didn't take part. Although it looked great fun and was well organized. I think the weather may have been a little rough on that occasion.

It must have been the year after moving to Herne Bay, 1980, when I again bought a boat. It was in no way a serious craft, being even smaller than the *Boat with No Name*, and it was also built of marine ply. The craft would probably have been more at home transporting gnomes across a garden pond. For all of that, it was light and easily carted about, making it ideal for teaching my sons the art of catching pneumonia and the occasional fish. We had no intention of going out beyond what was left of the pier, or in rough weather.

We had a couple of decent sessions on whiting and dabs. Even caught a few eels by the sewage outflow. This caused us to be over ambitious and enter the Dinghy Festival. On the slipway we heard a few disparaging comments about 'Idiots going out in balsa-wood boats,' but we had all of the safety gear and were not going more than a few hundred yards offshore.

We quickly realized that most competitors went out a couple of miles to fish. Things had changed since the sixties, and in the intervening years it looked like most of the fish had been caught, but then, north Kent was never going to be as good as fishing in the channel.

Come the weigh-in we still had a better catch from alongside the pier than some of the larger boats, who braved choppy seas and went out three miles.

The 'balsa-wood boat' was sold soon after that; possibly bought by someone who really wanted to transport gnomes across a garden pond.

I then bought a solid and seaworthy Norwegian boat made by a company called Alicraft. This led to a deal of confusion because it was actually made out of fiberglass. It had a powerful 18hp motor and could just about tow a water-skier—but not a fat one.

I was owed some time by my employers for time I had spent loafing about in airport departure lounges. This enabled me to take a few mornings off. My wife and I would breakfast early, take the boat to the slipway and skim away at top speed to somewhere like Margate spit. There was a deep channel alongside it where the fishing could be good. The problem was my wife started to out-fish me on a regular basis. One time she caught a 14lb thornback. I was never to catch anything that large off the north Kent coast.

On one occasion a friend joined us in another boat and we went as a flotilla, to Pan Sand, six miles out. I caught a bass weighing ten and a half pounds which was the biggest fish I was going to catch for the rest of my fishing career. But still smaller than the fish my wife had caught.

I used to dig my own bait, pursuing fat little lugworms through the claggy sand at low tide, with a fork or spade. Then I had to keep them alive. Using the family fridge for 'slithy' worms was against my wife's wishes, so I bought an old fridge for the garage.

When the worms were used they were subjected to unspeakable indignities, and, on occasion, even eaten alive by fish.

It was while bait digging, I started to suffer a tiredness I had not experienced before. Launching the boat also tired me out. It was time to sell it, with the idea I would buy another one when I felt fitter. After all, I was still only in my forties. Travelling all over the world I had little time to spare. On top of that I was planning to start my own business.

Most of the 1990s can be written off. I had a series of heart attacks, a stroke, and then a quad bypass operation just in time to save me. I entered the new millennium with a replumbed heart and a slightly scrambled brain—more of that in a later chapter though. However, I felt ready for anything.

I had been seriously interested in classic thirties cars and motorcycles for nearly fifteen years, having restored, first, a 1932 Austin Ten and later a 1939 Ariel

Square 4. Throughout my illness, I managed to stagger around the steam fairs and country shows whenever I felt well enough. I still had my two classics, and I now thought it time to build my very own Austin Seven Special to further increase my fleet.

A friend had an abandoned project from some forty years ago. We agreed a price and it all turned up on the back of a pickup truck. I could not wait to get started, although it lacked some of the smaller details. Like engine, gearbox, and a body.

However, the fun was going to be in building the body and sourcing the other components. I had used several large sheets of aluminium, and components from over a dozen different makes of car by the time it passed its MOT and took to the road in April '99. I hoped I had got it right, because I had booked it on an Austin Seven Club tour to Holland the following month. Having personally fitted every nut and bolt and connected every wire, I was sure it had to be right. Incredibly it was, and we had a mechanically uneventful holiday.

Such cars are great fun, but I needed something that would travel nearer to the speed of modern traffic. I had just built a larger garage so could just about find room for one, in addition to the two old cars and a motorcycle I still had. During a bout of irresponsible nostalgia, I bought a restored 1955 Standard Eight. A similar car to the one I had passed my driving test in, back in 1958. I had forgotten what a primitive car it was. My seventy-year-old Austin Ten was more comfortable.

I then started my last restoration project. A 1969 Austin Healey Sprite sports car. It was a long job as cars of that period rusted badly. A great deal of welding was involved but it was a lovely little thing when finished. We had a great holiday exploring Brittany with some friends in similar cars.

Chapter 31: Back to Freshwater Fishing

After years of sea fishing my lack of mobility in old age has forced me to consider freshwater fishing again. Sitting on a sunny riverbank, intently watching the float bob in the water would be pure nostalgia. The problem was, I fished for the pot these days, and hated giving grief or inconvenience to any fish that might be inedible.

Many freshwater fish can be eaten, but the rules state most must be returned unharmed. I really used to hate hurting the little fellows by disgorging a barbed hook. These days they no longer use these hooks, which was a deciding factor in my re-trying the pastime—purely for therapeutic reasons, you understand.

My son loaned me modern freshwater tackle and took me for a session at Marshside Lakes. Following this, my mind buzzed with how many things had changed since I used to fish regularly, back in the fifties. The bait for a start.

Everyone knows that fish are partial to the odd worm, and are also tempted by the occasional pellet, or crust of bread. I remembered it being such fun collecting the worms. Some were little red jobs from compost heaps. Then there were lobworms dug out of the potato patch, or nocturnal chappies that came out on to the lawns at night. No worm was safe from me at one time. If a trip was well planned, maggots—like smelly little animated concertina's—were bought from the angling shop. These baits had personalities, hopes, and dreams you could empathize with before throwing them in the water to be eaten alive by the fish.

Things are different now. Farmed worms have little character or personality and some of the maggots look positively dangerous. Luncheon meat or spam rarely fails to hook the curious and hungry fish... The poor little devils can't resist it would you believe? How could one possibly form a relationship of mutual respect with such a thing? I made the mistake of reading the contents of a tin once. I can't remember which processed meat it was, but it claimed to contain mechanically recovered pork. I immediately had visions of a pig being hauled, squealing, out of a ditch by a truck-mounted crane.

The actual meaning of 'mechanically recovered' I later found out to be even more grisly. Which, frankly, I'd rather not talk about. In mitigation, it makes up less than 50% of the tin's contents. Although sad about the fate of the porker's, which may, or may not, have had to dangle from a crane, the remaining 50+% of the tin's contents, caused me even more unease: *Diglycerides of fatty acids, maltodextrin, sodium erythorbate* and *sodium nitrate,* to name but a few. I'm no chemist but they sound like pretty ghastly things to dangle in a public waterway where an innocent fish or fowl might eat them.

But then—I had probably eaten them myself in the past.

The second bait recommended was sweetcorn. If they'd told me back in the 1950s that you could catch fish on it, I'd have laughed at them. Again, reading the list of contents on the tin, it proclaimed to be *salt free.*

Well, that's a step in the right direction. I'd hate the fish to get hardened arteries or suffer fluid retention. This must be a particularly embarrassing condition for creatures of an aquatic persuasion. However, what is it that is so familiar about the label on the sweetcorn tin? It portrays that huge greenish lout with the unpleasant smirk on his face. The words *Green Giant*, emblazoned above him? Didn't it used to be *'Jolly'* Green Giant? Why is he no longer jolly?

The rules stated that these strange baits had to be attached to a barbless hook and any fish was to have the 'hook removed while lying on a soft mat.' My initial alarm was lessened when I realized they meant the fish was to lay on the mat, not the angler.

The administrators of many lakes have put up a sign saying, 'No Boilies'. Boilies? What the hell are they? I had a *boil* on the back of my neck when I was a kid and it really hurt.

However, after some research, I believe they mean the little boiled balls of protein some anglers throw in to bait up the swim and attract fish. You can buy them by the sack at good angling shops I'm told. Whether these are responsible for these huge carp with distended bellies that some call 'Mud Pigs,' I wouldn't care to speculate. Perhaps these huge fish are just gluttons anyway?

Having dealt with some of the baits, I must now come to the subject of the tackle—from a 1950s dinosaur's point of view. A fixed spool reel back in those days was beyond the reach of many anglers, costing the equivalent of a week's wages, or more. Mitchell made the best ones as far as I remember, but there were a few cheaper substitutes available. I remember buying, for around nine shillings, one that relied on a rubber wheel making friction contact with a forward-facing spool. It would cast out well a couple of times. Then the friction drive became wet and the line twisted horribly. Hand-lining in was then the only answer. This was particularly difficult if you had a fish on the end.

A great deal better was a reel that looked like a standard centre pin, but had a spigot sticking out at the front, that you could transfer the spool for casting. It would then cast almost like a fixed spool reel, but not quite as well. I believe they were only meant for sea angling.

Back in 1949 I was bribed to do well in an exam by my grandparents. As a result of my marks I became the proud owner of a brand new Allcock's three-piece rod. This, joy of joys, had a split cane end section, the rest being ordinary cane. It cost £3.5s. which would be the equivalent of around £80 in 2022.

For years this rod cut swathes of misery across the freshwater fish population of the South East, from Shepperton Lock to the Royal Military Canal at Appledore. Sadly, it did not prove equal to tackling a lorry when it fell off my back while motorcycling down from London, years later. The split-cane end section was crushed beyond repair. I used a shortened version after that, and later still, the split cane section was replaced by the new wonder material—fibreglass.

I still have the remains of this rod somewhere. I've been intending to restore it for years.

Chapter 32: Surviving to the New Millennium

I was reluctant to leave the twentieth century. It was comfortable there and I had had my share of good times. However, in the end there was no alternative.

As I may have indicated in the previous chapter, the Grim Reaper had hung around throughout the nineties; he had probably made up his bed in the spare room, and seemed to jump out at me on every corner. I could have been forgiven for thinking that whatever the new millennium had in store for the human race, I would have no part to play in it. Besides all that, my brain had been scrambled by the stroke in 1996 and I could barely speak or write for a while. My only comfort was to think back to the good times, and there had been many.

Entertaining, and being entertained, is one of the few pleasures to look forward to at the end of the day when you have a stressful job. I liked exotic food and had eaten at some really good restaurants across the world. Often, I spent too long with customers or colleagues carousing the night away at *interesting*, if not slightly dangerous, downtown bars. Then, after little sleep and nursing a hangover, I would address the problem costing my employers so much for me to rectify.

I remember the excitement of a phone call from the head office asking me if I could be in Tokyo, or maybe Caracas, sometime in the next few days. However, the comforts of the occasional business or first-class travel never quite made up for the stress of getting to and through the airport. In addition, I always felt homesick after a couple of days. 'Make the most of it while it lasts,' I would tell myself, 'After all, someone else is paying for me to see the world.' I knew, deep down, that somewhere along the line, a personal payment would to be due. There is a well-known saying about there being 'no such thing as a free lunch'.

The bill came when I was in my early fifties, now running two of my own companies, and working long hours. It arrived on sheets of paper spilling noisily from an electrocardiograph, and indicated what my heart had, almost uncomplainingly, paid over the years.

"Bang goes the prospect of becoming rich," I told my wife, following an uncomfortable spell in hospital after the second heart attack. I was suffering angina attacks constantly and couldn't see how I was going to survive.

"The kids are off our hands and we would have moved to a smaller house anyway," she told me. "We'll get by. I certainly prefer it to being a rich widow."

The next few years proved rocky, and our savings were depleted rapidly as we tried to maintain the standard of living we had become used to. The situation bottomed out after I had suffered a TIA during an angiograph procedure at St Thomas's Hospital in London, which was being carried out to check my suitability for bypass surgery. The specialist showed me pictures of the blockages, telling me it was imperative I have a quad bypass soon, but fearing being unable to prevent me having a massive stroke during the operation.

'Well, I really wanted to hear that!' I thought, mulling over my death sentence. However, they assured me they would do their best. That was all I could ask. I had a couple of months to reflect on the slings and arrows of outrageous fortune. And get my affairs in order. They carried out the operation in mid-November after deciding it was time to get it over with one way or another. I did not have the stroke they were worried about, but things went badly anyway.

For about a week I entered a psychedelic hell of semi-consciousness and out of body experiences. There were mutants, and a tribe of marmosets constantly zinging about. Even a little train carrying doctors and nurses came chugging through the ward. Worst of all, I had concluded that many of the staff were bent on killing me. Earlier that week the operation had been done a second time.

When I look back, much of it was comical and a product of my over-active imagination reinforced by drugs. However, my humour and sense of the ridiculous was stretched to the limit by the physical discomfort of having my chest opened up twice, even though I knew nothing of it at the time. It was almost two weeks before I became aware, again, of the real world. It looked good and I wanted to re-join it.

I believe my recovery proper began with a tuna sandwich. The first thing I had eaten since entering the hospital. As I enjoyed It, I was able to look out of the window for the first time and see Big Ben smiling benevolently at me. I couldn't make out the time though.

Then I remembered giving my glasses to my wife for safe keeping. I had hoped the less I could see of what was going on, the safer I would feel. It hadn't worked out that way because what I couldn't see clearly, I had made up in my imagination. That probably accounted for the marmosets and mutants I had seen. I wonder what they really were.

St Thomas's hospital sent me home at the beginning of December, only for my own doctor to send me straight into Canterbury hospital with a pulmonary embolism. I remember thinking, 'My cup runneth over.'

I am inclined to think this was the Grim Reaper's last vain attempt to get me before the new millennium, but I was out of hospital in time to celebrate Christmas 1997. The following two years I pottered about in the garage building myself an Austin Seven Special. The idea was to get my brain and hands coordinated before returning to work proper. I still had hangovers from the stroke in early '96, which affected my speech and writing. A large slice of my vocabulary had disappeared completely. Reading at every chance was the only way of renewing it.

I finally returned to the family firm after years of tussles with the angel of death. I was now sporting a re-plumbed heart, slightly jumbled brain, and a resolve never to take life seriously again. The years that followed until my retirement passed pleasurably. I enjoyed my work and followed a healthy lifestyle.

My last overseas assignment was to appear as an expert witness, in a lawsuit between a US company and a Chinese company. I had promised my family, and myself, I would never again put myself in a stressful position. I had not expected it to be stressful, thinking I knew my stuff through and through. However, years of illness and the ravages old age had taken their toll. I found myself in a Hong Kong hospital with heart failure. I was there three days and afterwards, foolishly attended the tribunal to defend my report. I did not do well against the legal eagles.

I felt like kissing the ground on disembarking from the 747 after landing at Heathrow. I had travelled on a plane for the last time.

I heard some years later we had actually won the case, but that was no consolation. I had to retire in 2005, I was 67 years old.

Chapter 33: Surviving Retirement

My time was now my own; how would I use it? We had bought a retirement bungalow. It had room to build a four-car garage alongside the house, where I could while away what time I had left, tinkering with old cars and motorcycles.

The bungalow was a little pokey and old-fashioned, needing extensive work. Although I intended to spend all my time in the garage my wife needed somewhere comfortable to relax and do her arts and crafts. She enjoyed cooking as well at that time.

We looked at expensive kitchen units and building alterations. Then the summer cabin erected in the garden for her to do her handicrafts. I foolishly told myself that all the expensive work would see us out, lasting for the rest of our lives. I was wrong.

I started to go deaf as I reached my early seventies. This made arguing with my friends increasingly difficult, and arguing with people who were not my friends well-nigh impossible.

As the hearing loss further increased, my social life started to decrease and I could only console myself with the thought that my flatulence, another unwelcome feature of old age, was now less noticeable. To me anyway.

In a crowded bar I would mishear things and give responses that had my friends rolling with laughter. Sadly, at times the thin dividing line between them laughing with me or at me became difficult to define.

Being unhappy at this I acquired a pair of hearing aids. These allowed me to hear the birds singing in the trees again, which was nice, but did little for holding conversations in a crowded room. I still found it hard to differentiate between the words of the person I was talking to and a conversation going on behind me. Whoever had the voice best attuned to my limited frequency range would win out. In a restaurant or bar it would usually be some harpy singing for her lost love over the speaker system.

Otherwise, my seventies passed pleasantly enough. I returned to sea fishing and became quite enthusiastic about it, although it had become exhausting and painful. My fishing pals then started to fall off the perch—as did other friends.

Life was becoming like a battlefield. So, before I have to take my turn in the box, I decided to research the family history. The idea was to leave some sort of record behind me while there was still time. My Aunt Jackie had just died, leaving me with a load of family photos. Many I did not recognize, and a few I didn't want to.

Although still suffering slight cognitive problems as an after effect of my stroke, back in '96. I thought it might be fun to enrol for some creative writing lessons. There was only so much I could learn from re-reading, 'Eats, Shoots, and Leaves.' I would always now be rubbish at punctuation, possibly a legacy from the stroke affecting my timing. Or a developed stupidity I could not overcome. I never have got around to writing a proper family history.

This book is as near to one as I'm likely to get because there would not be enough laughs to keep me interested.

I grew to love writing for the sake of writing, and have written hundreds of short stories and the best part of three novels. They all live on a memory stick tucked away in a drawer somewhere. No one has read them or is probably likely to.

I was up early on my birthday. I rolled out of bed and painfully staggered a few yards to grab a pair of tracksuit bottoms. "I'm eighty years old today and I have lived longer than any other male member of my family," I said to the mound under the covers on the other side of the bed.

"As if the world did not have enough problems! Many happy returns old git!" a muffled voice replied from beneath the mound. Then I accidentally caught sight of myself in the mirror. This was something I tried to avoid as much as possible.

'I look like a duck,' I wailed inwardly, trying in vain to hold myself in and reduce the large wobbling shelf of flesh concealing my once flat stomach. The rest of me was quite slim, which made it look even worse. I cast a longing glance at the wardrobe containing the smart suits I wore a few years ago. 'Life can be bloody unfair,' I thought.

However, looking on the bright side, many of my family reached a point in their old age when they became thin. I shall keep the suits and try to ignore the fact that their thinness came just before falling off the perch.

The unfairness of life has always interested me as I hoped constantly the dice may fall in my favour.

But the regular gambling of hard-earned money doesn't do any good, as fortune only favours the fortunate. I'm not a gambler.

One of life's greatest misfortunes must be having to eat boiled cabbage. Cabbage is a particularly vengeful vegetable that will jump out on the unfortunate and slither on to their dinner plates, if not kept in its place—which is on the greengrocer's shelf.

As I have mentioned before, the tons of high explosive falling around me in WW2, whilst still a young child, paled into insignificance compared with the danger of having cabbage served for dinner. It seems even stranger now I'm old, that a vegetable should be the only thing that had really frightened me in the mayhem and carnage of wartime London.

I have gone on about cabbage extensively throughout this book, and I apologise, but it has always been there, its dark presence threatening me for over eighty years now. I promise I won't mention it further.

In spite of my age and list of infirmities, life is still fun for me. Perhaps because now I don't take myself, or life, too seriously. I have an interesting and memorable past, in a minor sort of way, but my future in the 21st century does not promise a lot more laughs. There are few of my old friends left now. Some have moved away; others became no longer fun as the boredom of retirement and senility robbed them of their sense of humour. The rest, sadly, are dead.

Finding the local Micropub was a godsend for me. It was only a mile away, had no music or gaming machines and using a mobile phone got you fined or thrown out. I would turn up at lunchtime in order to be the first customer. Then have a normal and enjoyable conversation with two or three regulars, until the bar filled up. After that, if the noise made conversation difficult, I would drink up and go home for lunch.

Sadly, consuming alcohol no longer makes me feel good and a pint of bitter has to be paid for with an entire afternoon asleep. Being conscious of how few afternoons I may have left, I'm now loath to squander them in this fashion. I really miss going to the micropub.

The one thing I wanted to do was go fishing. There was no substitute for it as I had persecuted fish since catching my first one in 1946. There would have been no question of giving it up, even at 80, but for the arthritis in my spine. The ailment had made its unwelcome appearance a couple of years after my deafness, progressively reducing my walking ability to a few yards. "It's about the only thing they can't fix with a new joint these days," the doctor had told me.

No one could accuse me not a being a pragmatist. Such problems I see as a challenge to be overcome, and perhaps give scope for some fun and mild geriatric hooliganism. Rumours abounded as to the contents of the big box the neighbours had seen delivered. Had the old sod purchased his own coffin, I could imagine them wondering. My views on the cost and formality of funerals were well known. Eventually, they would find out that I had bought an electric mobility buggy. The sort that could do an illegal speed, rather than the more restrained shopping sort that will only crawl along at 4 mph.

My intention was to modify the buggy for fishing. This necessitated a frantic spell of hobbling around in my workshop, waving spanners, screwdrivers, and using intemperate language. It made my back hurt but I was prepared to suffer for my art. The modified buggy, when unveiled to an unappreciative public, sprouted things that looked like the smoke canister launchers fitted to battle tanks—but most would accept my assurance they were fishing rod holders. A box for the fishing tackle, beer, and other refreshments graced a bracket behind the seat, and a tray on the front carried the unspeakably horrid things I used as bait. I had deliberately arranged these to be in full view of anyone with a weak stomach, and out of the reach of passing dogs.

It had occurred to me to tweak the motor control circuits to make the buggy even faster, but the condition of the pavements made this unwise. Even hitting a piece of uneven tarmac at 10 mph could throw me off into the road. I also resisted the temptation to drive the device on the roads as many other buggy owners did, realising it could put me in the position of victim. An altercation with a pedestrian or pushchair was one thing but arguing with a bus could be painful. Furthermore, I had a couple of perfectly good cars for that sort of thing.

The place I wanted to fish was Bishopstone. Two miles from home at the bottom of some cliffs. However, there was no direct route. It meant crossing a flyover, where the pavements were broken, and crossing a bridge over a railway track. I also had to pass the micropub, which could increase journey time should I be thirsty.

One overcast Thursday, when the tide was just coming up to high, I unloaded the buggy from my car, and drove it down the twisty path to the concrete breakwater. This was a place I had not been able to visit for years since arthritis set in. Driving carefully towards the edge I found a six-foot drop on to the shingle. I feared that if I staggered about trying to fish from there, I was likely to fall over the edge.

There was a slipway nearby so I drove halfway down it to where it could be considered safe to cast out my line. As often happened on such fishing trips, I found myself baiting up, casting and waiting vainly for bites. Frequently I lost hooks and sinkers amongst hidden rocks as I tried to wind them in. If I did succeed in winding in without mishap, I found the crabs had stripped the hooks of bait. It was a rotten place to fish. However, I was enjoying every minute of it.

Disaster struck as I attached my last piece of squid to the hook and cast it out. My hands were covered in the ripe smelly squid I was using as bait, so I wiped them on a piece of towelling I had brought for this purpose. Then I tucked it between the buggy handlebar and operating lever. Normally this would have been a good place to keep it if I had remembered to switch the buggy power off.

In my excitement of finally getting a line into the water, I had completely forgotten.

The buggy powered up and leapt forward, hurtling the remaining short distance down the slipway and burying its nose in the shingle at the bottom.

I had been sitting side-saddle facing the sea and was carried along for a way, then thrown face down onto a pile of rotting seaweed. Then, to add insult to injury, the back wheels continued to turn showering me with shingle. All I could do was ponder my misfortune and glare at the buggy from my prone position, until a large pebble thrown up by the spinning wheels hit me on the tip of the nose.

It was only then that I found the energy and resolve to crawl over and switch the power off.

One misfortune is often harbinger of another in my experience, and true to form a dog appeared and noticed the lugworm bait box where it had fallen on the beach. The poor little fellows were crawling from it, hopeful of reaching the sea, and salvation. The dog woofed them down as if they were sweeties. I had no more suitable words for the occasion, so I just lay alongside the buggy, put my head in my hands, and groaned.

The dog owner had seen much of the accident from a distance. He called his dog to heel and rushed up to give assistance, probably thinking I had surely been killed or gravely injured by the fall from the buggy. However, as he drew closer, I was just picking myself up.

"That lug-worm cost nearly five bloody quid a score and your dog's eaten half of them," I said ruefully.

Apologies made for the repellent gluttony of his dog, the walker then dragged the buggy out of the shingle, helped me back into the seat, and trotted behind me back to my people carrier, where I and the buggy were safely loaded aboard. I thanked him profusely, assuring him there would be no charge for the lugworm eaten by his dog.

I staggered into my house, fragile and exhausted.

My wife greeted me with heavy irony. "Will I need the large frying pan?"

My reply was terse.

"When are you going to admit you are too old and disabled to do these things?" she asked. I envisaged the few lines somewhere on the inside pages of the local paper.

'Disabled pensioner drowned in buggy fishing horror. Coastguards warn against driving electric buggies into the sea. No fish were harmed.' I hoped my departure from this life would be a little more dignified than that. I had visions of me and the Grim Reaper chatting companionably as he led me off towards the setting sun.

Perhaps I will become a writer instead of a geriatric adventurer. Now, where did I see that pencil and notepad?

Acknowledgements

I am grateful to my wife, Hazel, for having put up with months of communication in the form of impatient grunts, while I tapped feverishly away on my keyboard; my son, Stuart, for his original artwork depicting Coulthurst Cottages in Streatham, featured on the cover; my grandson Oliver, for the rest of the cover design; the encouragement of the rest of my family and members of various writing groups too numerous to mention; and, last but not least, my editor, Karen Ince, without whom publishing the book would never have been attempted.

Printed in Great Britain
by Amazon